Oron Tal

"11"

Paintings and Drawings

2010-2012

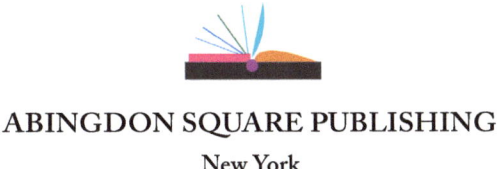

ABINGDON SQUARE PUBLISHING

New York

ORON TAL
"11"
PAINTINGS AND DRAWINGS 2010-2012
is published by
Abingdon Square Publishing Ltd.
463 West Street, Suite G122
New York, NY 10014 USA
www.abingdonsquarepublishing.com

Book Design: Abingdon Square Publishing
Cover Art: *The Lady in the Café* © Oron Tal, 2013

The author gratefully acknowledges permission to reproduce and reprint the following material:
"Letter From the Consul General of Israel in New York" by Ambassador Ido Aharoni, Consul General
"Beit Issie Shapiro Certificate" by Beit Issie Shapiro

And to reprint the following articles:
"Preteen Artist Sells Art for Good Cause Copyright" © 2012 by Josey Bartlett/Queens Chronicle
"Oron Tal "11" Exhibition" Copyright © 2012 by NY Art Beat
"Oron Tal "11" - Paintings and Drawings" Copyright © 2012 by The Queens Courier
"Art Exhibit To Benefit Special Needs Children's Charity In Israel" Copyright © 2012 by FIOS 1 Long Island

Photographs of the exhibition, pages 92 – 97 and page 12 and the Back Cover by Arturo Amaya

ISBN 978-0-9830762-4-7
Library of Congress Control Number: 2012945582

Printed in the United States of America

For Mom, Dad,
Val, Andrea
For being there for me,
And all my friends who cheered me on…
I dedicate this book to you.

ACKNOWLEDGEMENTS

Marcia and Naftali Tal thank the following people for enabling the success of Oron's art exhibition:

Valentina DuBasky for her unwavering commitment to, and belief in Oron as a gifted artist and unique young man. Thank you, Val, for all the "teachable" moments and love of the arts you create for Oron.

Andrea Piccolo for her continuous support of Oron. Thank you, Andrea, for your vision, design, professionalism and publication of this outstanding book as a memoir of Oron's first art exhibition.

Richie Amity, of Amity Studio, for his creativity and professionalism in matting and framing all of Oron's artwork. Richie's insights and commitment to Oron's exhibition were invaluable.

Juan Gabriel, and the M55 Art Gallery, for providing a beautiful and welcoming gallery for Oron's exhibition.

Peter Weiss, and Prestige Caterers, for ensuring that the gallery was continuously filled with beautifully designed, delicious food and drinks.

Ed Ward and Beit Issie Shapiro for their support of Oron's art exhibition and their partnership in the success of this event.

Jason Mandella for photographing Oron's paintings and enabling this book to be created.

Arturo Amaya for photographing and "catching" the wonderful experiences of the day.

Solomon Schechter School of Queens community for their generous support of Oron's art exhibition.

The Tal's family, friends and community for their generous support of Oron's art exhibition.

TABLE OF CONTENTS

CATALOG OF PAINTINGS AND DRAWINGS

INTRODUCTION

It was December 2009 and I had just received an email from a colleague about a talented eight-year-old boy who loved to paint and draw. His parents were looking for an art teacher for him and I was intrigued by the thought of meeting a young boy who loved art and so I invited Oron and his mother, Marcia, to a gallery exhibition that I had organized in New York City. Oron was excited to be at the show and walked around the gallery looking very carefully at each of the paintings on the walls. I could see that he was thoughtfully engaged with the artwork. I could tell that he was a very intelligent young man who was passionate about painting. I agreed to take him on as a student.

Our lessons were conducted at my artists loft in the West Village in New York City, where Oron would gain firsthand experience creating art in a real working artist's environment. He would be in a space that was enriched by art – making art, looking at art, reading about art, and always, discussing art. From the very beginning, Oron loved to draw and paint and I could see his potential that was very exciting. His creative output flew on the wings of his prodigious imagination. He always came to class with several ideas for paintings he wanted to make and often completed two or more paintings during class. Through his art, Oron explored ideas, made connections between things, solved artistic problems, described his experiences, created imaginary worlds, and responded to the master works of famous painters. I introduced him to books in my art library – including those on Botticelli, da Vinci, Matisse, Chagall and Modigliani and soon he had established his own relationships with these historical and contemporary artists and was taking out books from his local library on Botticelli to read at home.

Each idea that Oron brought to class represented a teachable moment for him to learn about new methods, techniques, and materials. He has explored watercolor, pen and ink, collage, conte crayon, pencil and acrylic techniques with enthusiasm. He worked on paper, board, canvas, panel, silk, and vellum. His homework included visits to museum shows in New York City, which feature some of the most important art exhibitions in the world.

The process of training a gifted and talented child, who dreams of a life in the arts, does not happen in a vacuum. It can only be realized if his parents are committed and dedicated to his artistic education and are willing to make sacrifices to support him. They first have to recognize a special gift possessed by a child that often appears as an aptitude, an interest, or the urgent necessity of a child to create, and then dedicate themselves to the task of his ongoing training. In this regard, Marcia and Naftali are exceptional parents. They recognize Oron's artistic talents and want to help him achieve his desire to become an artist. They understand that Oron's talent needs to be met by education and training, and their support of Oron during these early years is crucial to his development as a young artist. Even if Oron decides to choose a path other than art, the training has instilled in him a valuable approach to life, and a deeper understanding of himself that will inform and strengthen his future choices.

It is my belief that the practice of educating a young artist is built on the ongoing consistency of regular lessons over time. Oron came every week for his art lesson and no matter how busy the Tal's were with other activities or family obligations, or how bad the weather was or how difficult it was to make the drive into the city, Marcia and Naftali made sure that Oron had his weekly art lesson.

After the first year of art lessons Oron had several themes or subjects he liked to paint and had developed many paintings representing his different interests. The idea for Oron to have an exhibition of his paintings and drawings came to me one afternoon when I was listening to a young musician's concert on a New York radio station. These talented young musicians who had undergone a period of intense training were given a moment to perform before a public audience that was beyond the classroom environment. Was there anything like this for young painters? Although schools present artwork by students, and there were some juried art competitions for young people, I could find no comparable opportunities for young painters to have an experience of this kind. Dancers could perform with a goal of gaining professional experience early on with a company, young actors could find opportunities to move beyond the school play, and exceptional young athletes could work toward the Olympics. All of these young people were prepared by a combination of ongoing training and public performances. There seemed to be nothing like this for young artists. Although creating art is a very personal experience, the prospect of taking his artwork into the world enabled Oron to develop new skills and confidence.

Oron's exhibition was understood as a learning experience. I presented the idea to Marcia and Naftali who were excited about it and brought their dedication and commitment to the project. Oron was very excited. So we got to work. Over the next year, Oron learned how to develop a body of work for his exhibition. He learned how to critique his artwork, reflect on his development so far, make decisions about what to do next and follow through on his commitments. He gained the knowledge of how professional artists prepare for an exhibition of their artwork, including curating, framing, and installing a show. He learned how to talk about his art with audiences of all ages.

Most importantly, Oron learned firsthand about the larger role of the artist in society – how art can enrich communities and create a dialogue and how artists can be of service. Oron decided to donate the proceeds from his show to Beit Issie Shapiro, a charity he visited in Israel that helps children with disabilities. Marcia, Naftali, and I are very proud that the sale of Oron's paintings has made a difference in the lives of children in need.

I am equally proud that Oron created so many beautiful paintings for his exhibition on the various themes that are represented in this book. As an artist and his teacher, I have watched him learn, struggle with issues, deepen his understanding, broaden his skills, and explore his creativity. We have many interesting discussions about the wonderful and mysterious world of being an artist. This book represents the paintings and drawings he created during his first two years of private art lessons with me.

Oron is eager to move forward with his art. He is now 11 years old and ready for a new year in which he will be working on developing his portfolio for admission to art school. He has recently finished his first oil painting, a larger project that has involved advanced planning and preparations and that is usually undertaken by much older students. He is already thinking about his next exhibition.

– Valentina DuBasky
  New York, 2012

M55 GALLERY EXHIBITION INVITATION

ORON TAL

"11"
Paintings and Drawings
2010-2012

Reception
May 20, 2012
From 12 - 6 pm

M55Art
44-02 23rd Street
Long Island City, NY 11101
718-729-2988

Proceeds from sales will benefit Beit Issie Shapiro

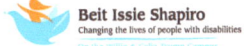

Beit Issie Shapiro
Changing the lives of people with disabilities
On the Willie & Celia Trump Campus

Beit Issie Shapiro named #1 most effective charity in Israel

The Lady in a Cafe, 2012, 12 x 9 inches, Acrylic on paper

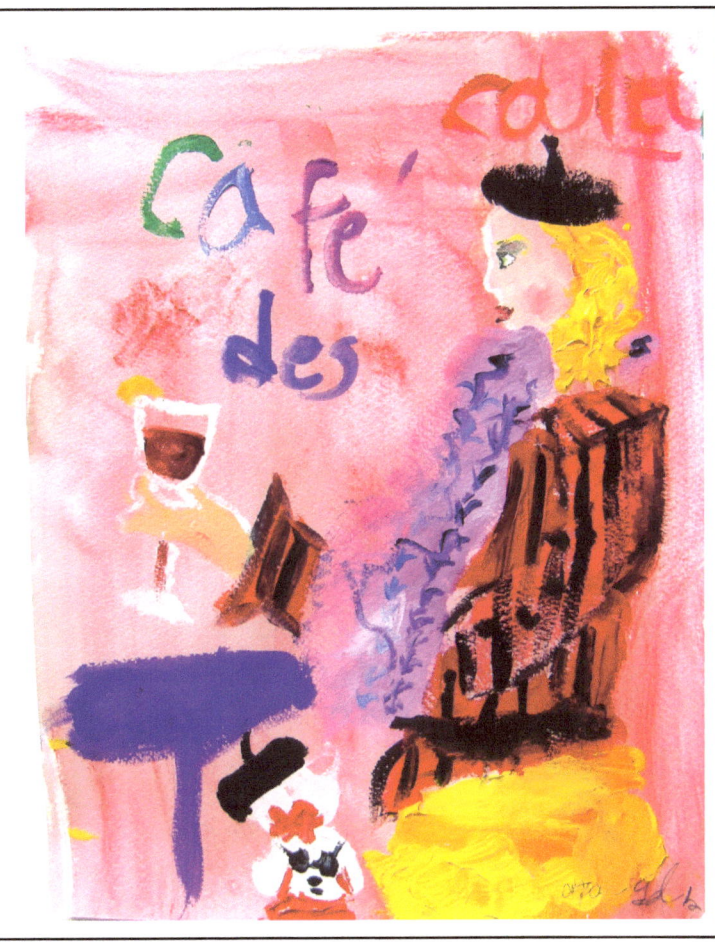

M55 Art Press Release

FOR IMMEDIATE RELEASE

"11"
Paintings and Drawings, 2010-2012
By Oron Tal

Artist Valentina DuBasky is pleased to present her student, Oron Tal, age 11, in his first solo exhibition. This exhibition titled "'11' Paintings and Drawings, 2010-2012" will take place at the M55 Gallery on May 20, 2012, 12-6pm. In 2010, Valentina accepted Oron, then an eight year old student, after recognizing his passion for art. For two years, he has been coming to Valentina's painting studio in the West Village in New York City for weekly art lessons. This exhibition marks Oron's first two years of art study with a selection of paintings and drawings in a variety of media on the themes of travel, reading, media, fashion and family.

Valentina is an exhibiting artist whose work has been included in more than 150 exhibitions nationally and internationally. She is also the founder and Executive Director of Art-in-a-Box, an international nonprofit organization. Oron's artwork has been influenced through a combination of Valentina's unique expertise, Oron's diverse experiences, his rich imagination and love of learning. Oron writes of his relationship to art:

> *"Art of any kind makes me feel happy and excited. In fact every day I make sketches of nature, places and people I imagine. I get pleasure in designing the facial expressions, hair and clothing of these people. Occasionally, these sketches are developed into paintings, drawings, and nib work. Many of my own experiences become part of my work."*

Oron Tal is a student at Solomon Schechter School of Queens. Oron's academic environment is a place where curiosity rules and where children learn to honor timeless traditions and think for themselves. The students are encouraged to become global citizens – the classroom is a launching pad that enables students to view the world from an extraordinary new perspective. Oron's artwork projects his global lens and the recognition that we are all part of something greater than ourselves.

Being a global citizen encompasses a commitment to social responsibility – a call-to-action as compassionate human beings. **Oron will be donating proceeds from the sale of his artwork to Beit Issie Shapiro, Israel's most effective nonprofit organization in 2012.** Beit Issie Shapiro is a leading innovator of new therapies for children and adults with disabilities, sharing best practices internationally. Beit Issie plays a leading role in promoting the inclusion of people with disabilities in society. Oron is happy that his art can help people in need and invites all to join him in supporting Beit Issie Shapiro.

Oron's show, "'11' Paintings and Drawings, 2010-2012" presents 50 original works of art that demonstrate the breadth and depth of Oron's creativity, intellect and skill in expressing his ideas and interpreting the world around him. Please join us to celebrate the beginning of a unique creative journey of a young artist.

Letter from the Consul General of Israel in New York

**CONSULATE GENERAL
OF ISRAEL IN NEW YORK**

CONSUL GENERAL

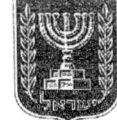

הקונסוליה הכללית של
ישראל בניו יורק

קונסול כללי

May 15, 2012

Mr. Oron Tal
Hollis Hills, NY 11427

Dear Oron,

I take this opportunity to personally congratulate you on your upcoming exhibition at M55ART in Long Island City, in support of Beit Issie Shapiro.

As you well know, the children and adults living in Israel with disabilities are in constant need of our support. It was a pleasure to hear that you have taken it upon yourself to do what you can for those less fortunate than us. As an artist, you are in the unique position to inspire and touch countless lives through your medium. Not only will the proceeds of your art go towards helping these individuals, but you bring much needed awareness to this cause and to this wonderful organization. I have no doubt you will inspire others to do what they can for those in need. I am sure that your family and friends are proud of your talents and achievements.

On behalf of the State of Israel, I wish you all the best and much success on this exciting occasion. I am sure we will see many more wonderful things from you in the future.

Sincerely,

Ido Aharoni

Ambassador Ido Aharoni
Consul General

Permission to reprint courtesy Ambassador Ido Aharoni, Consul General of Israel in New York

BEIT ISSIE SHAPIRO CERTIFICATE

 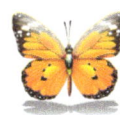

Dear Oron,

בית איזי שפירא
לשינוי באיכות חייהם של אנשים עם מוגבלויות

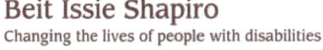

Beit Issie Shapiro
Changing the lives of people with disabilities

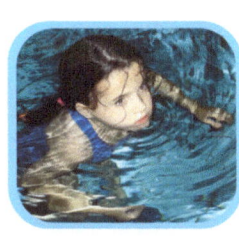

MAZALTOV on your successful first art show and a huge THANK YOU for supporting the children of Beit Issie Shapiro!

You are clearly a talented young artist, with a great sense of leadership and compassion. May you continue to be a source of joy and pride to your family, and may you continue to absorb and express the Jewish values of community, chesed (loving kindness) and tzedakah.

With much love and thanks,
the children and staff at Beit Issie Shapiro
and our American Friends

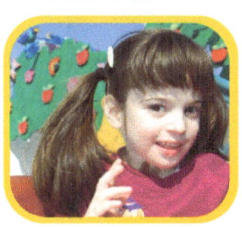 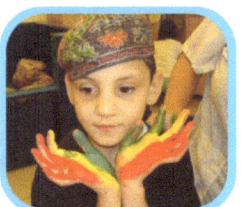 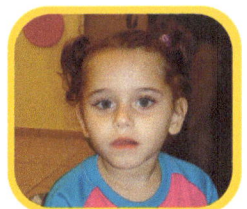 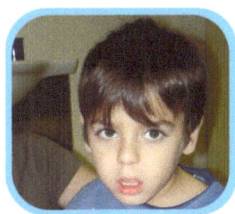

Permission to reprint certificate courtesy Beit Issie Shapiro

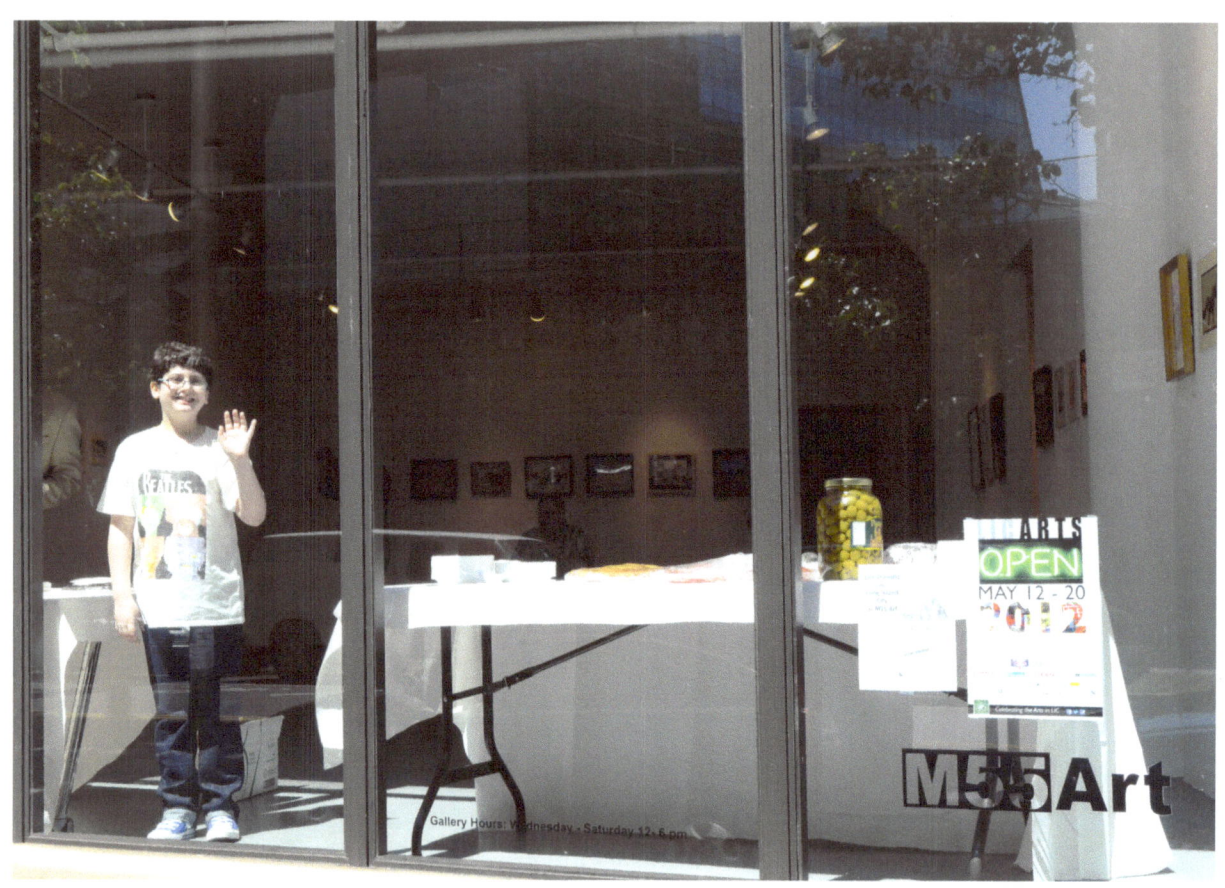

Oron Tal at the M55 Art Gallery   *Photograph by Arturo Amaya*

ARTIST'S STATEMENT

Art of any kind makes me feel happy and excited. In fact, every day I make sketches of nature, places and people I imagine. I get pleasure in designing the facial expressions, hair and clothing of these people. Occasionally, these sketches are developed into paintings, drawings, and nib work. Many of my own experiences become part of my work. For instance, when I traveled to Paris, I visited the famous Café de Flore, known for its atmosphere, not food. I sat and watched the people in the café and know how the French love dogs. This café had made an impression on me and I created a Parisian lady and her outrageously dressed dog sitting in the fictional Café de Couleur. I have also done nib work in the past two years. My nib work is included in my show.

My art lessons with Val bring my art work to new levels. She encourages me to study various artists so that I can learn about different styles and materials.

– Oron Tal
  New York, 2012

The Peoples of Chagall (after Chagall) (detail)

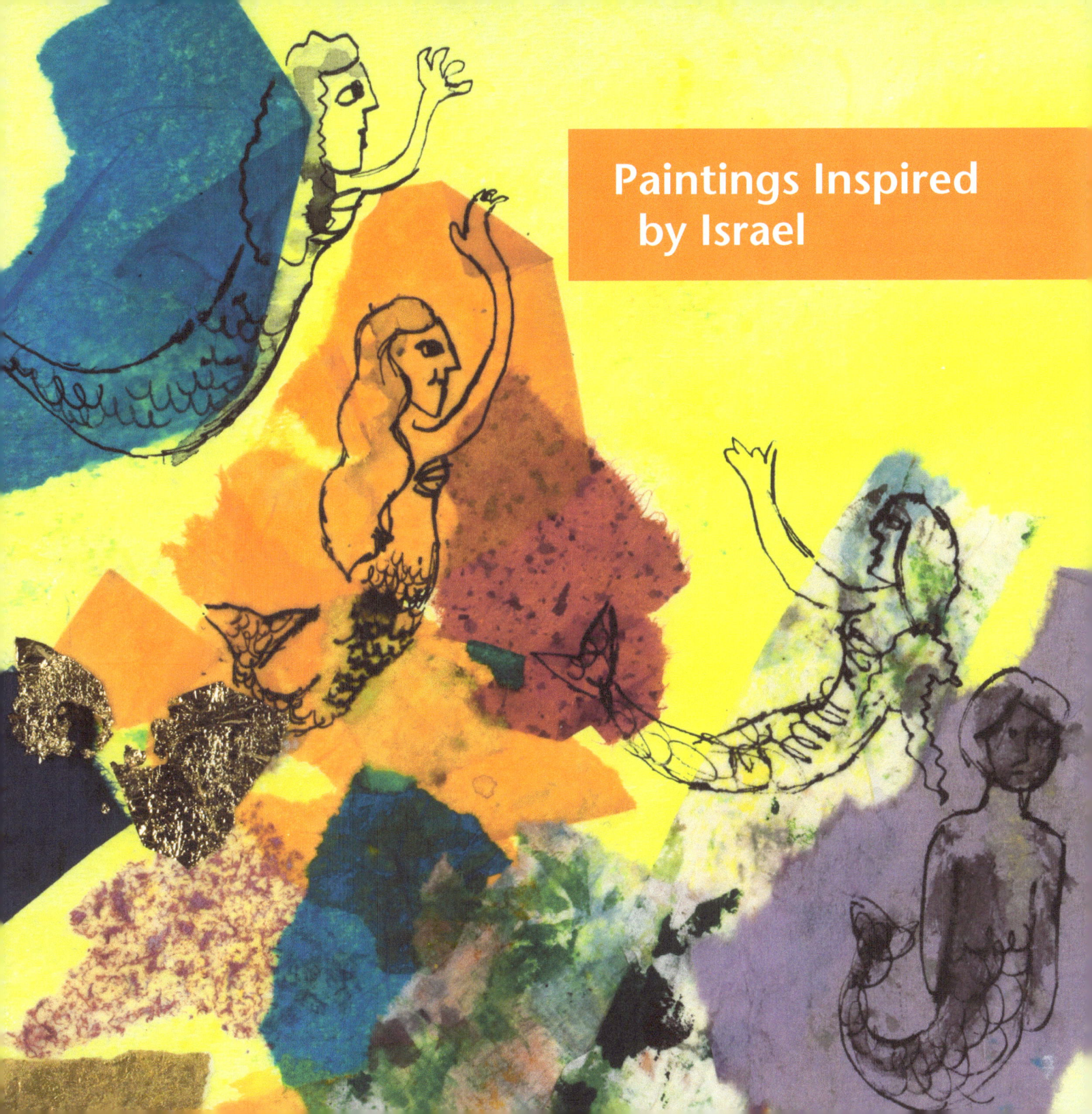

**Paintings Inspired
by Israel**

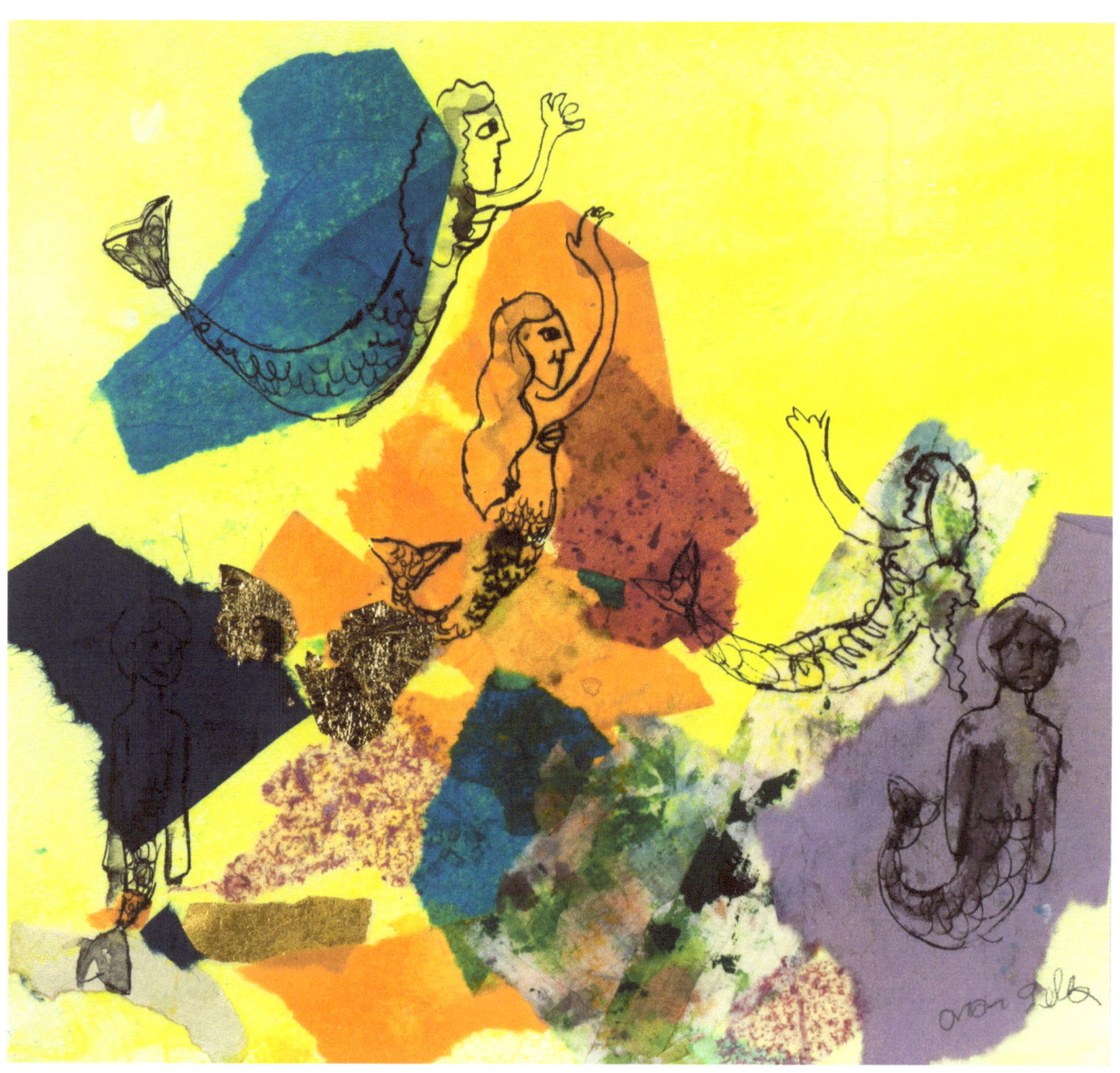

The Peoples of Chagall (after Marc Chagall)
Acrylic, ink & collage on paper, 10 x 10.5 inches
2012
Courtesy of Jessica and Laurence Sheinman

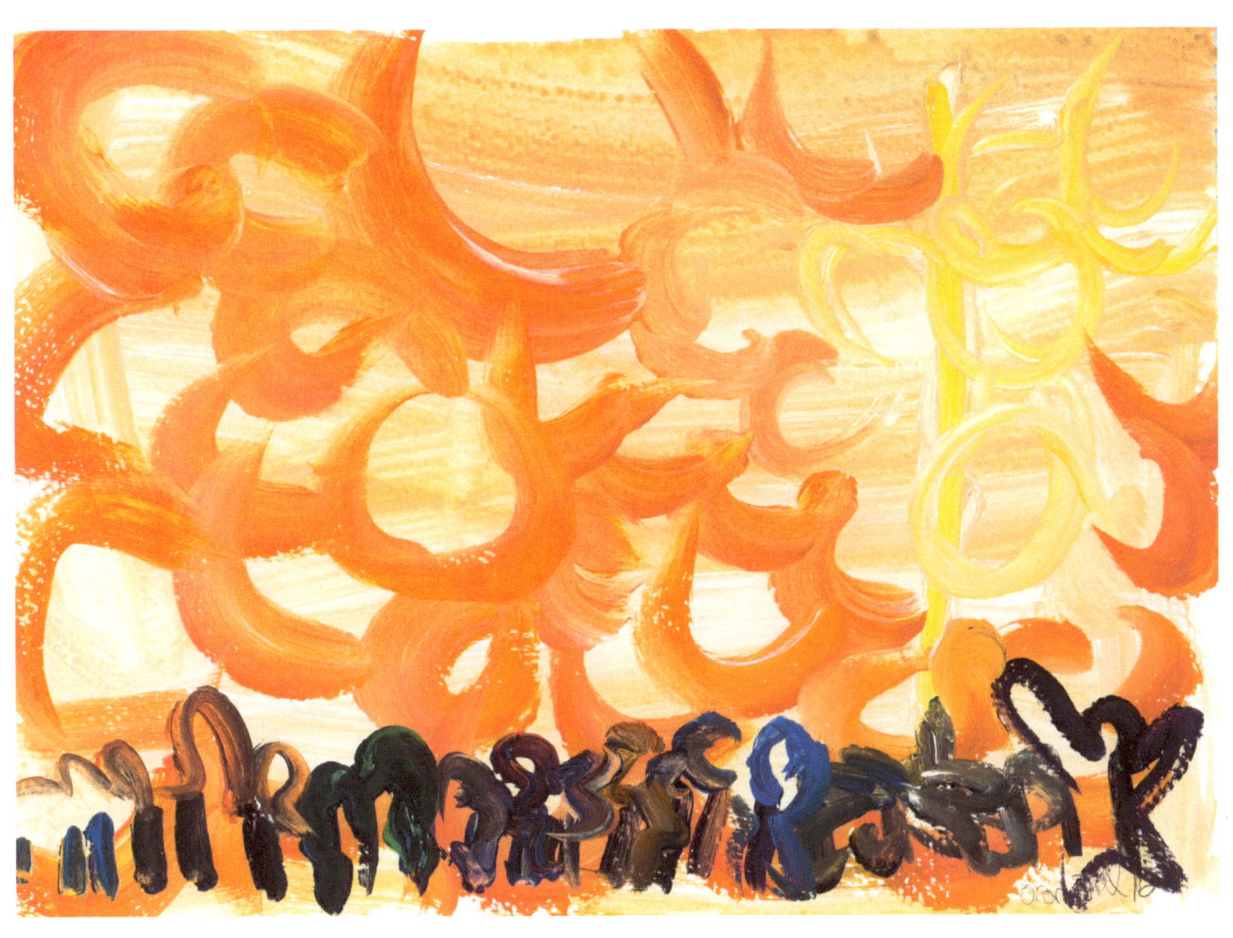

Wailing Wall
Acrylic on paper, 9 x 12 inches
2012
Courtesy of Marilyn and Stan Seidenfeld

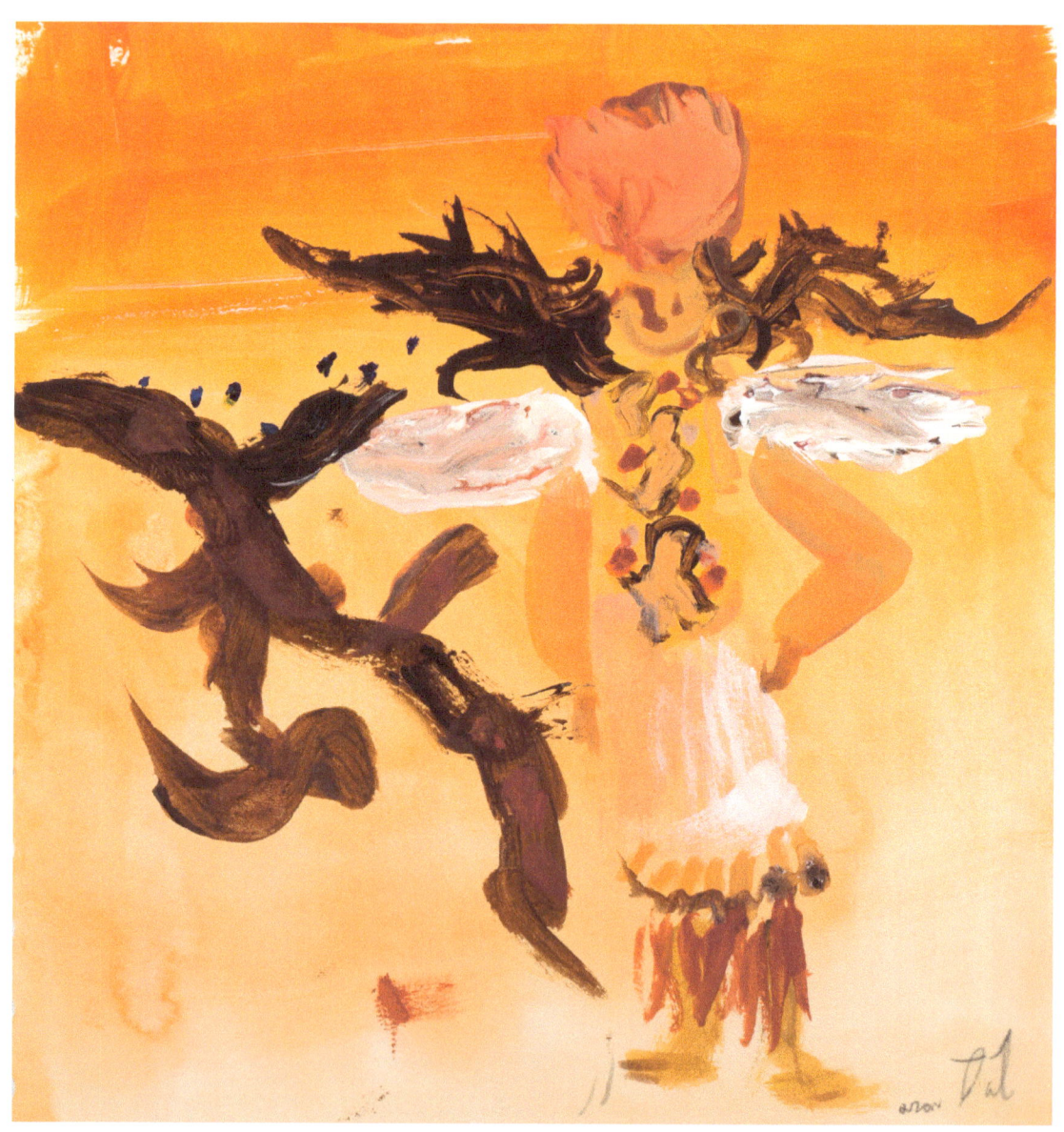

Greek Daphne in Israel Bird Dress Hoopoe (1 of 3)
Acrylic on paper, 7 x 6.5 inches
2011
Courtesy of Marge and Guido

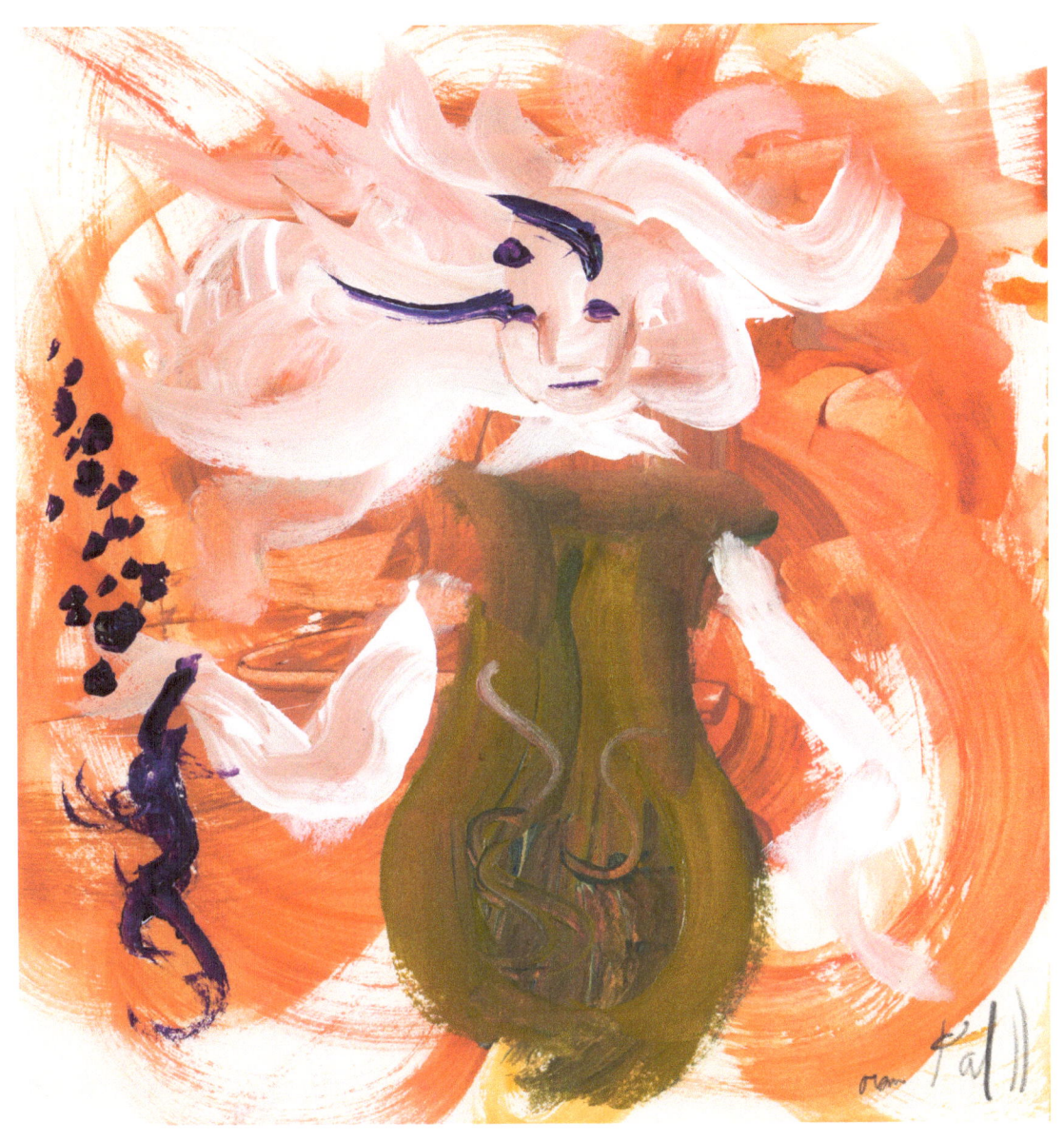

Lady with the Hidden Face and Cyclamen (2 of 3)
Acrylic on paper, 7 x 6.5 inches
2011
Courtesy of The Zabib family

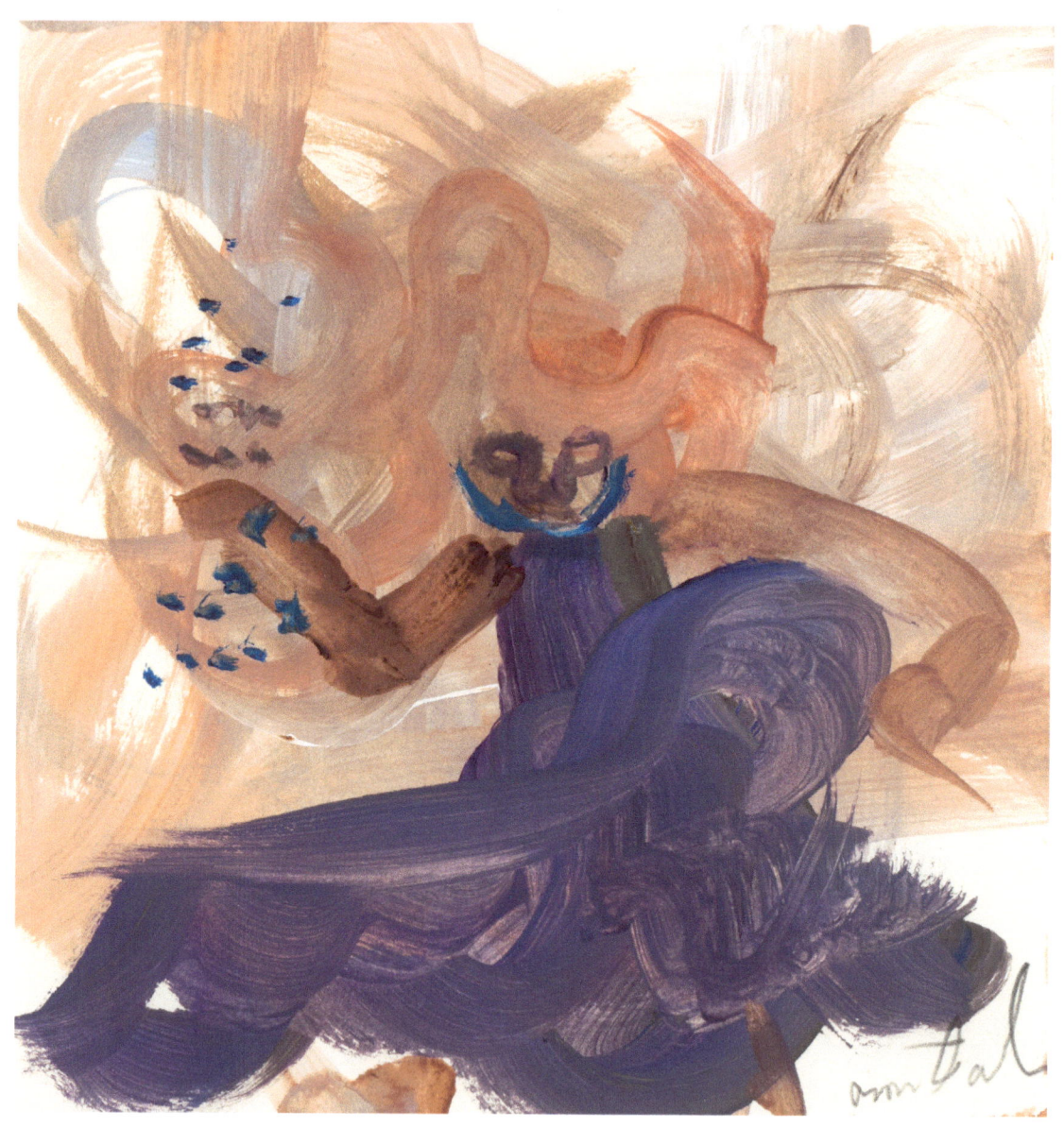

Lady with the Hidden Face and Blueberries (3 of 3)
Acrylic on paper, 7 x 6.5 inches
2011
Courtesy of Judy and Randy Stein

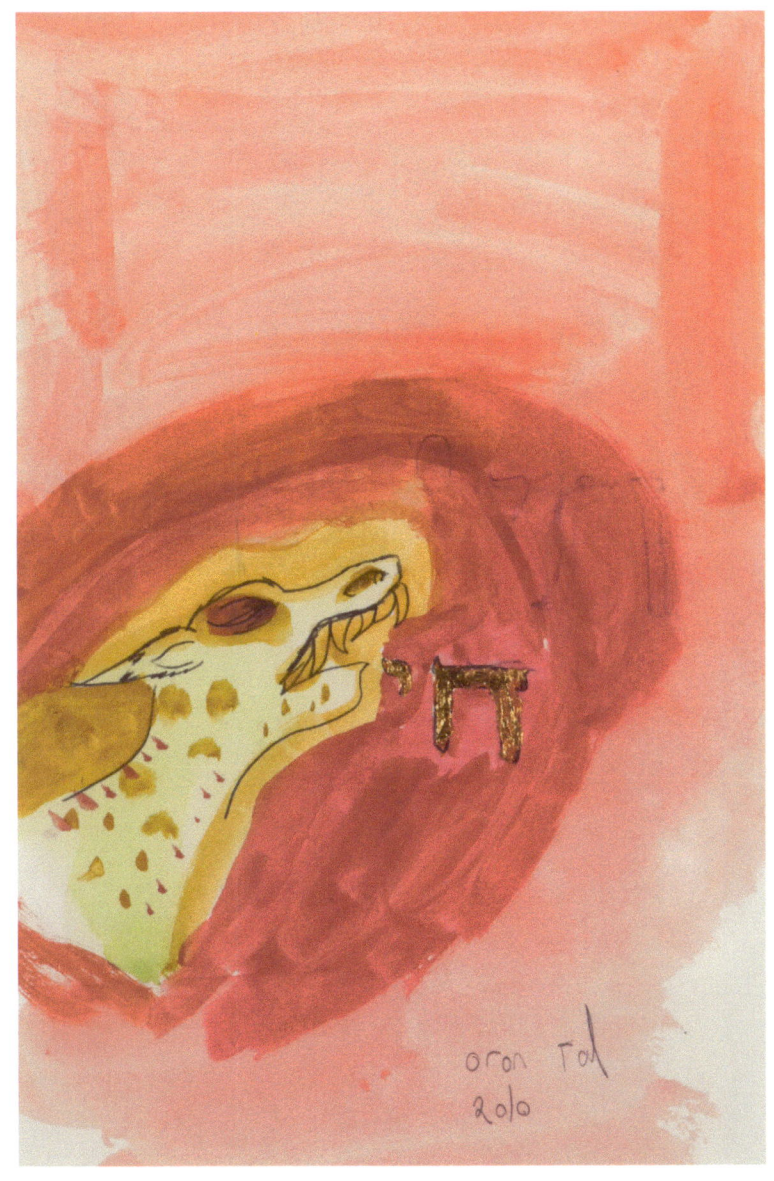

Untitled (after Ben Shahn)
Watercolor, gold leaf and ink on paper, 10 x 6.5 inches
2010
Courtesy of Marcia and Naftali Tal

Untitled (Adele) (detail)

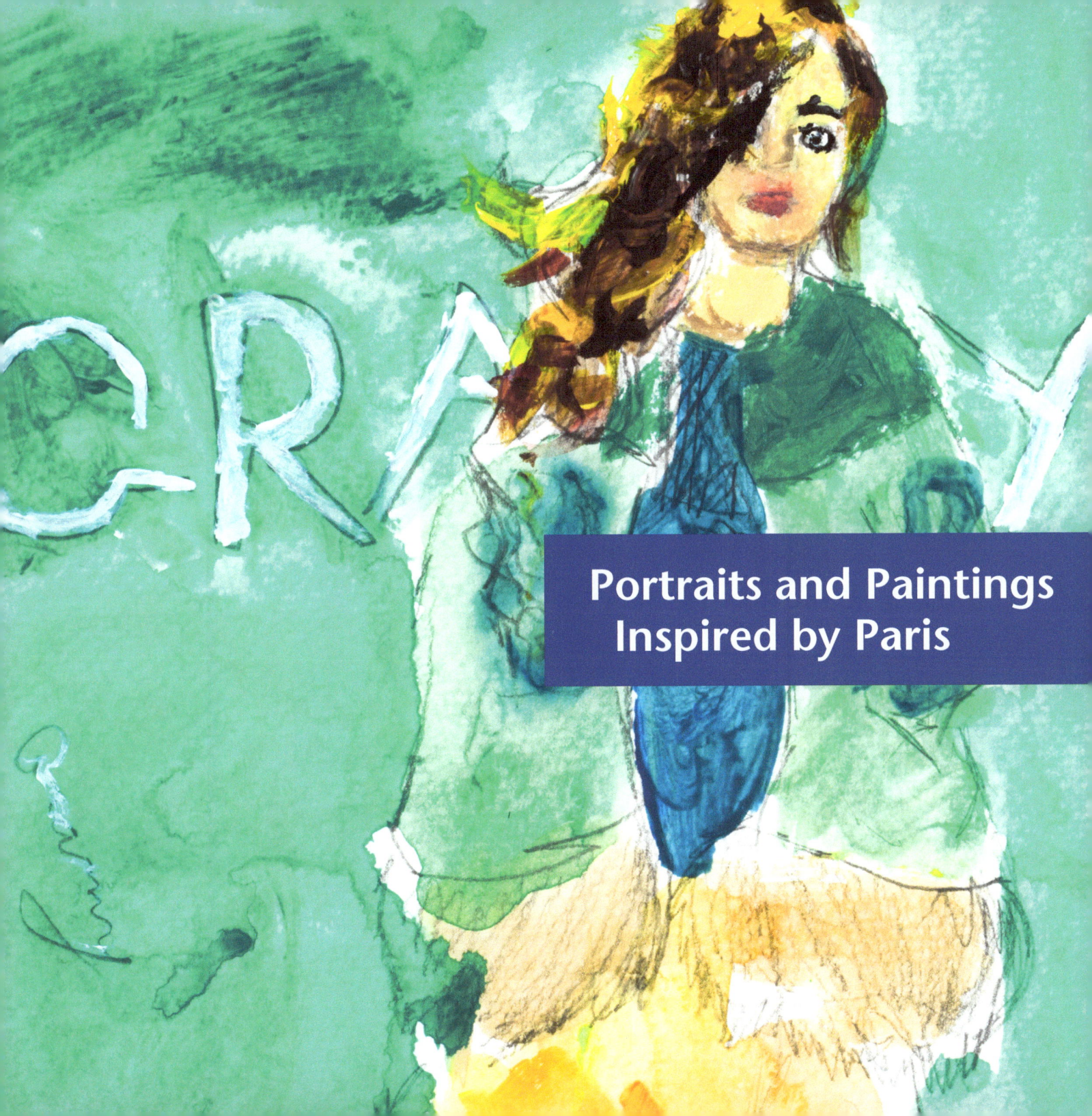

**Portraits and Paintings
Inspired by Paris**

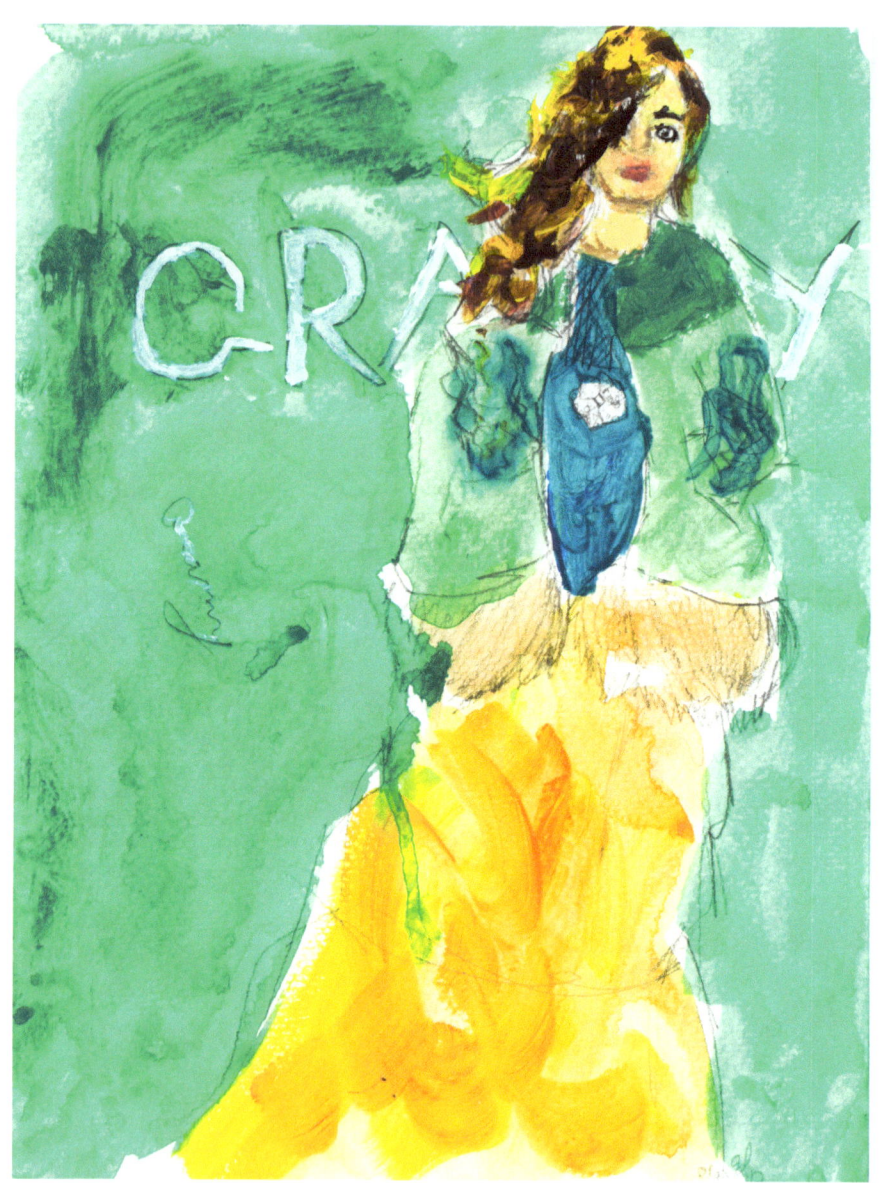

Untitled (Adele)
Acrylic on paper, 12 x 9 inches
2012
Courtesy of Terri and Walter Winter

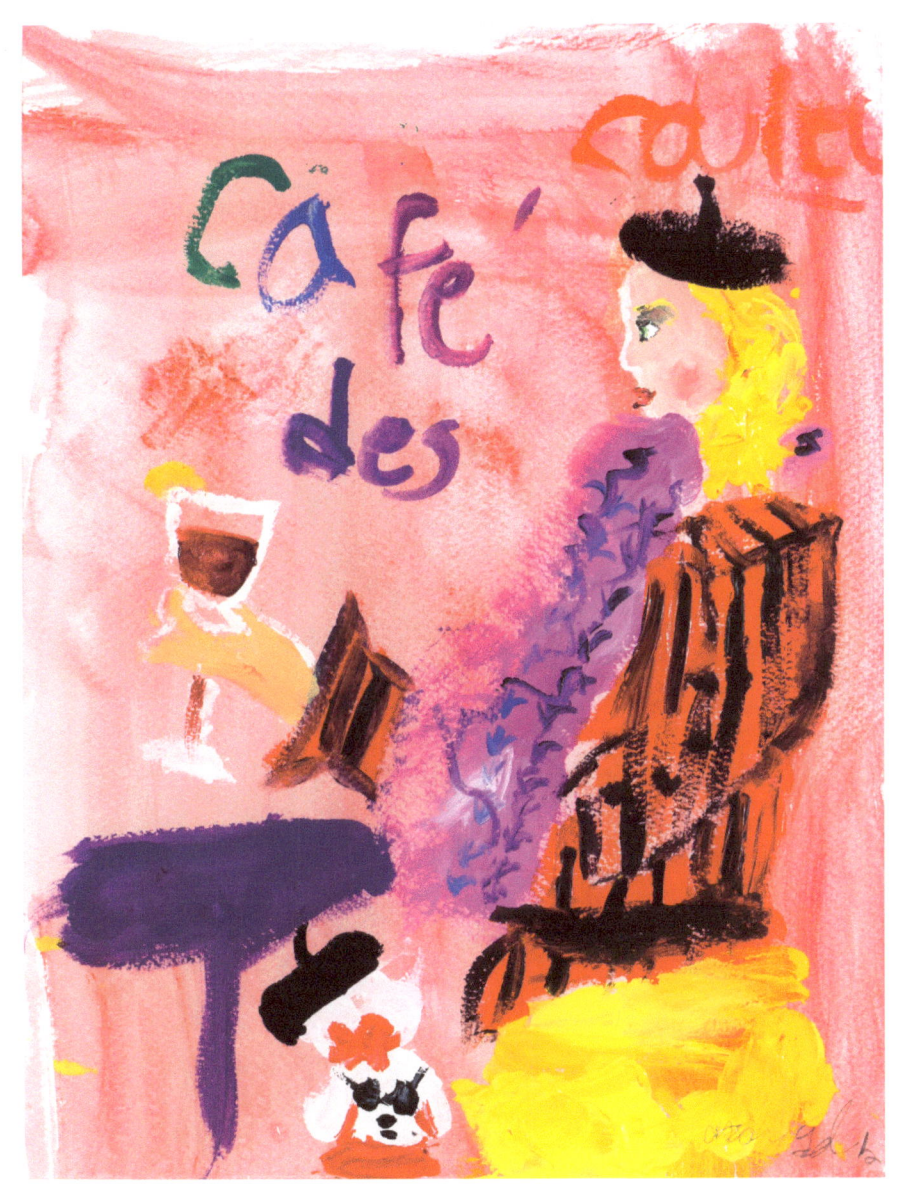

The Lady in the Café
Acrylic on paper, 12 x 9 inches
2012
Courtesy of Cari and Jeffrey Schnipper

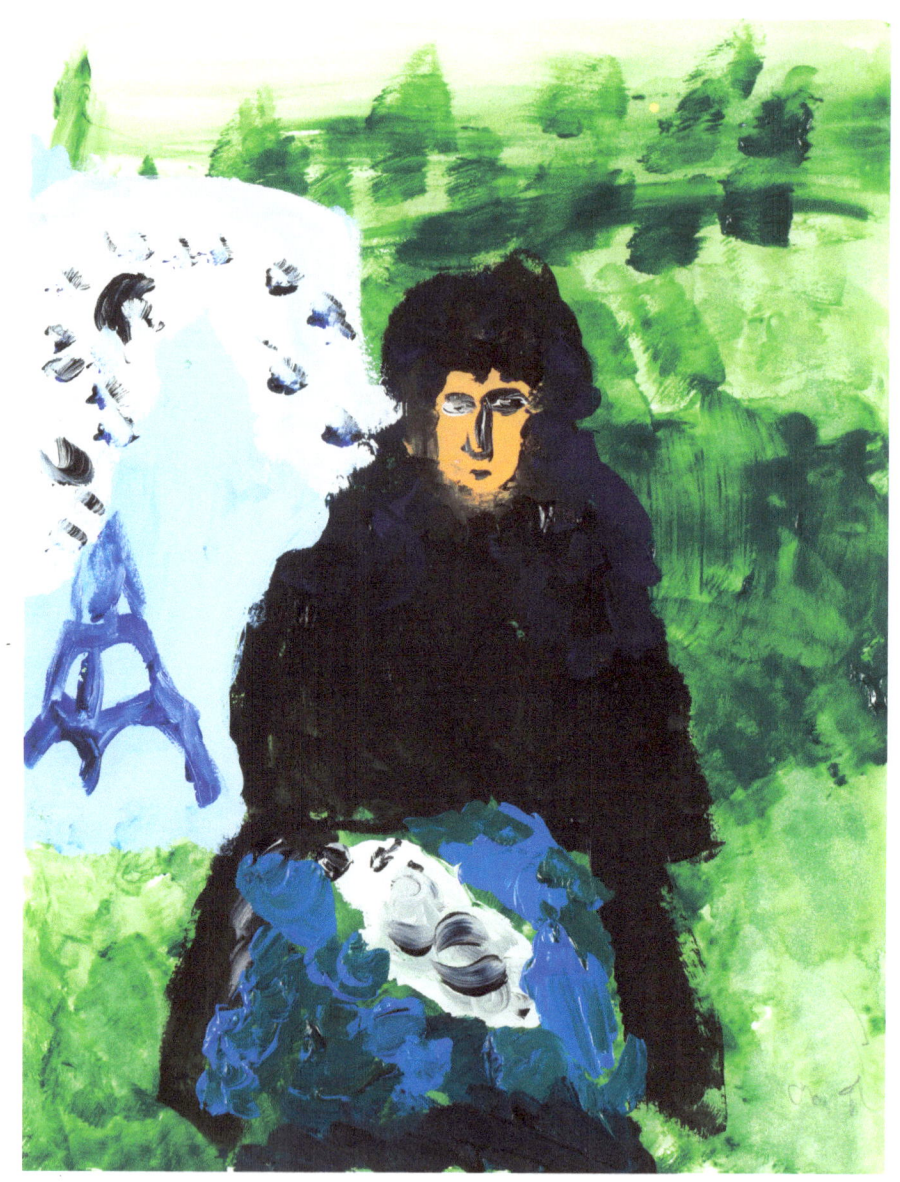

Lady, Dog, Eiffel
Acrylic on paper, 12 x 9 inches
2011
Courtesy of Yessenia and Jose Gomez and family

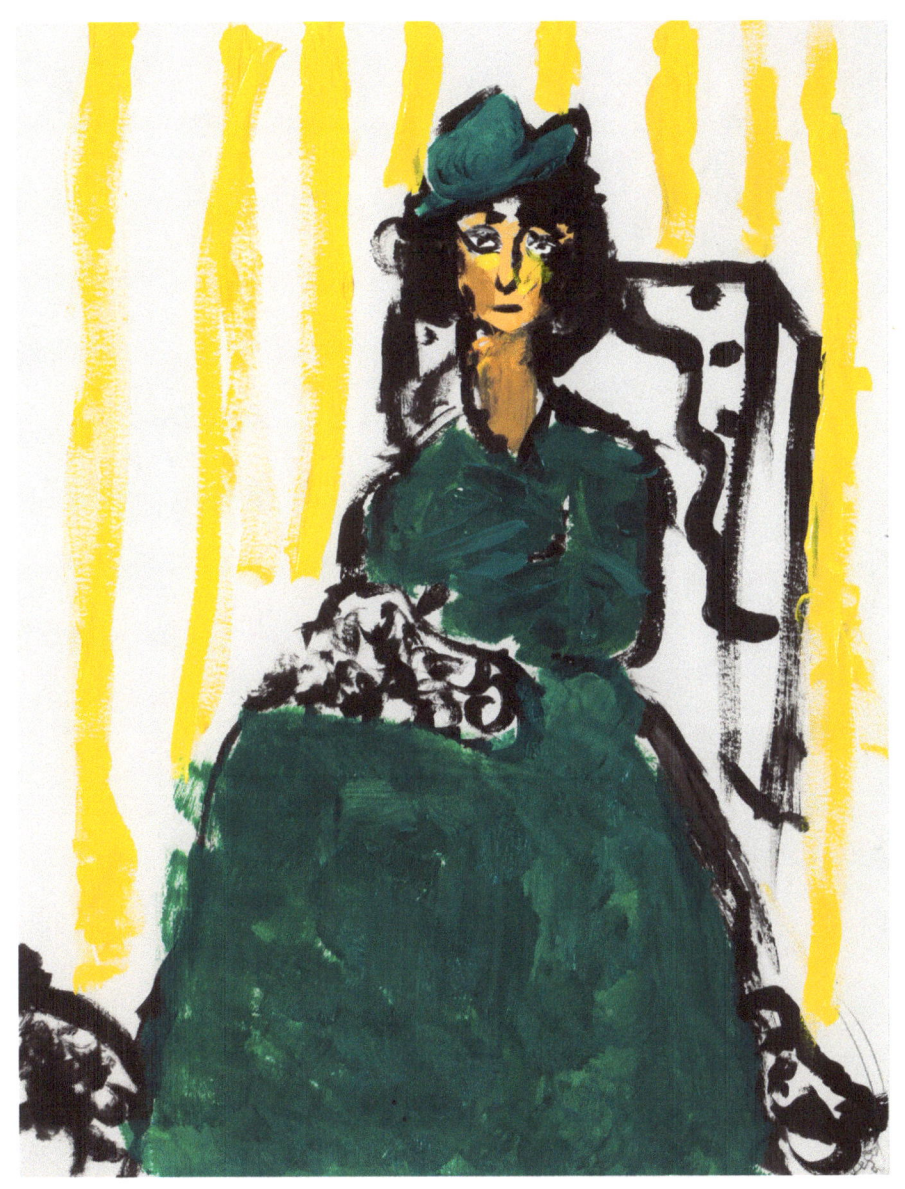

Lady and Dogs (after Henri Matisse)
Acrylic on paper, 12 x 9 inches
2011
Courtesy of Marian and Sheldon Naparstek

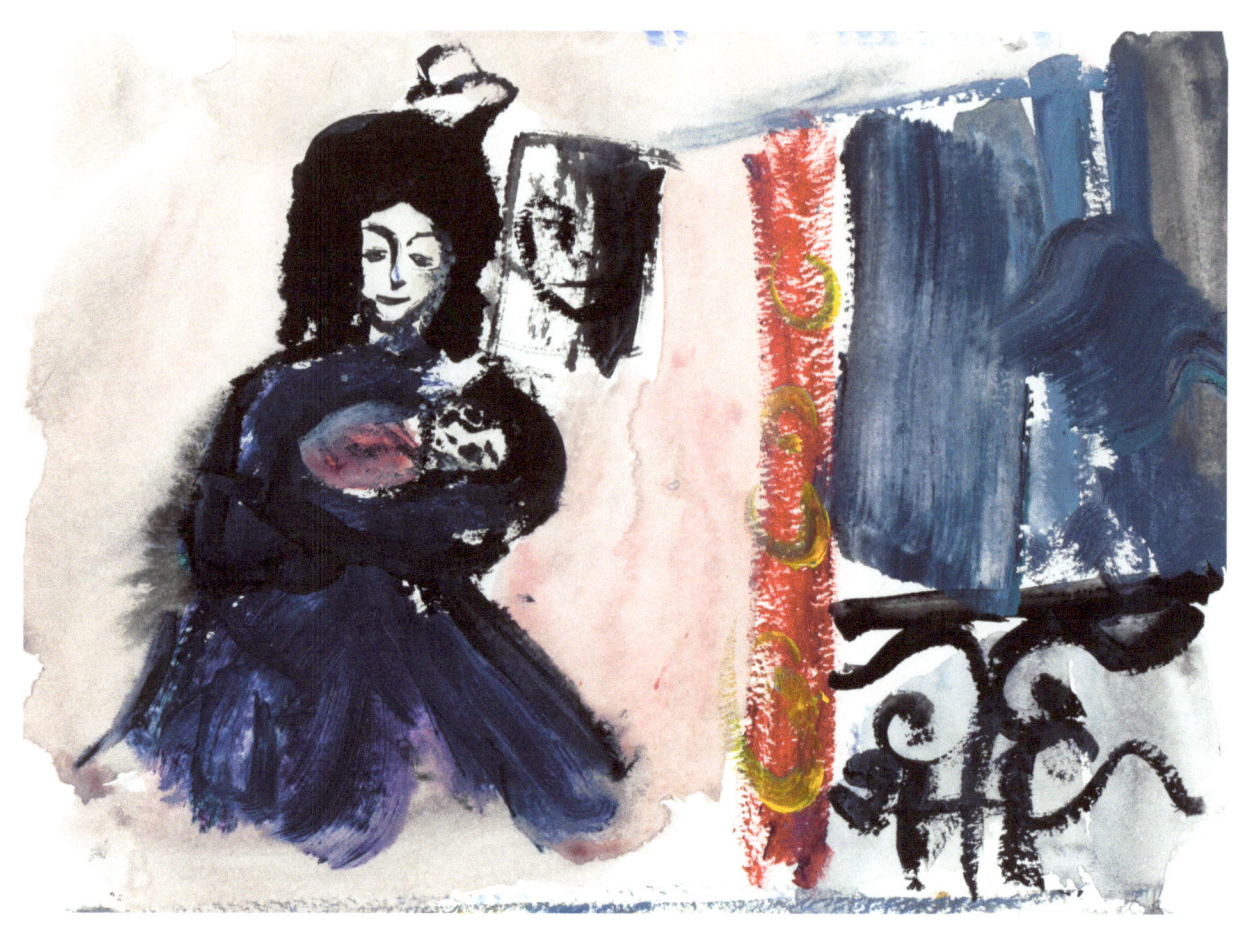

Lady with the Baby
Acrylic on paper, 9 x 12 inches
2011
Courtesy of Randi and Harry Weinberg

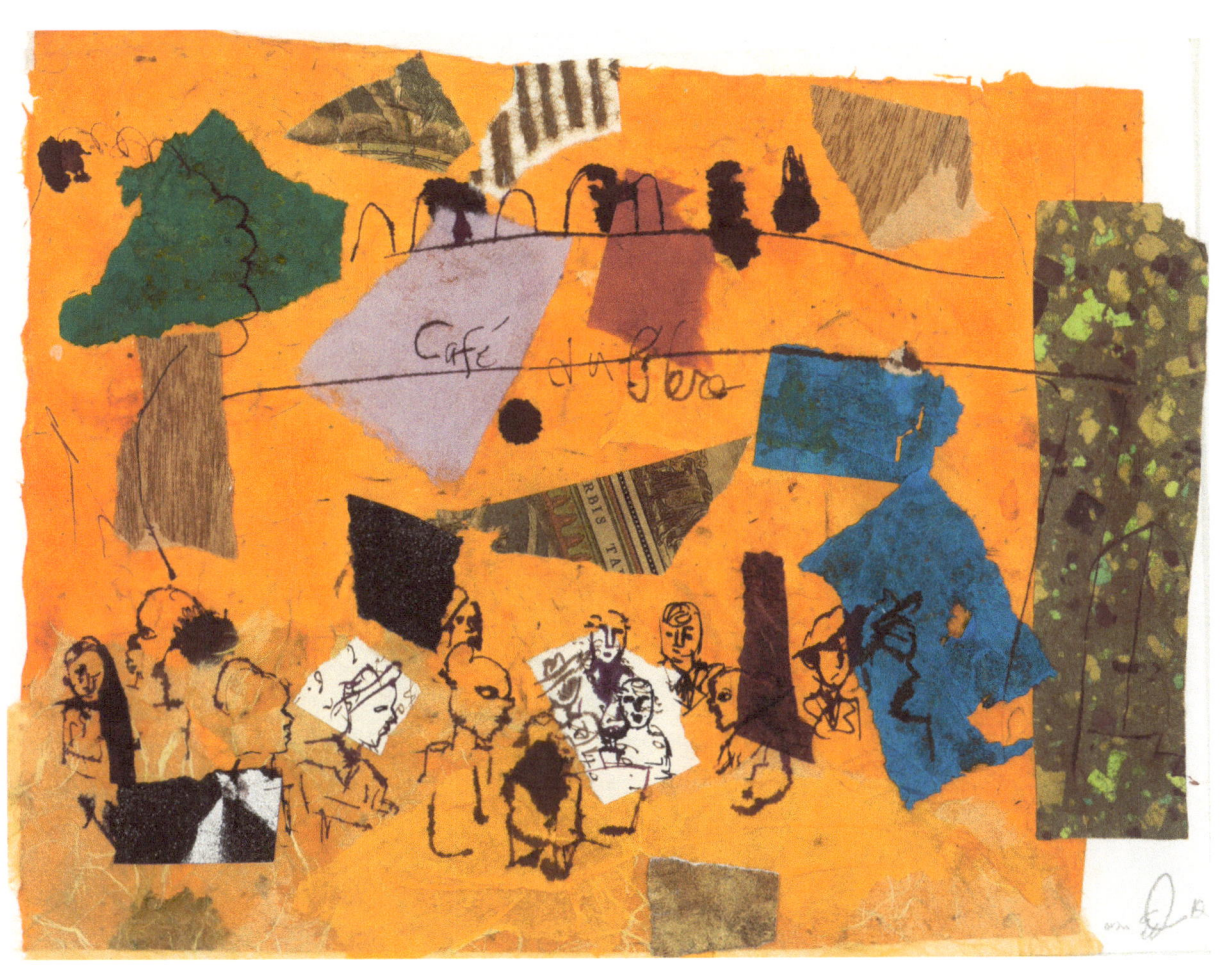

Café de Flore
Acrylic, ink and collage on paper, 9 x 12 inches
2012
Courtesy of Marilyn and Stan Seidenfeld

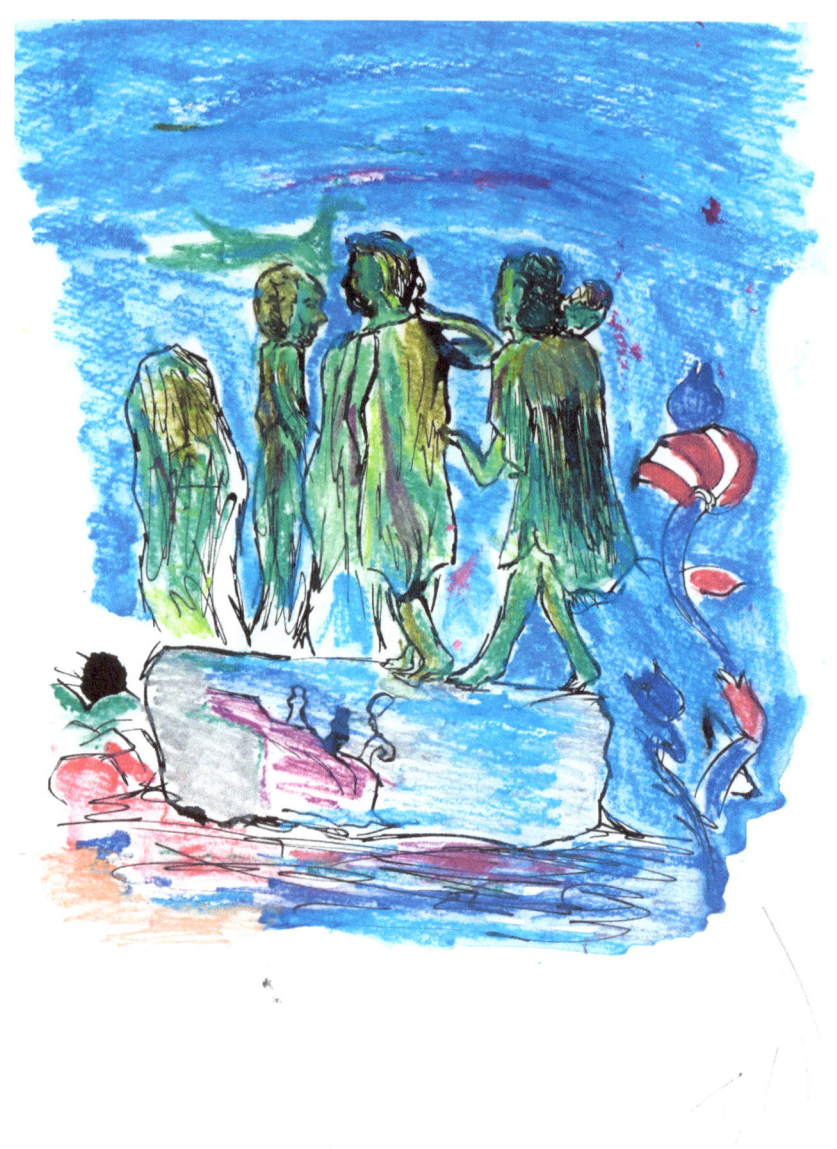

Rodin's Garden de la France
Ink, watercolor and pencil on paper, 7 x 6.25 inches
2011
Courtesy of Phyllis and Victor Merriam

Lady Gaga Clothes (detail)

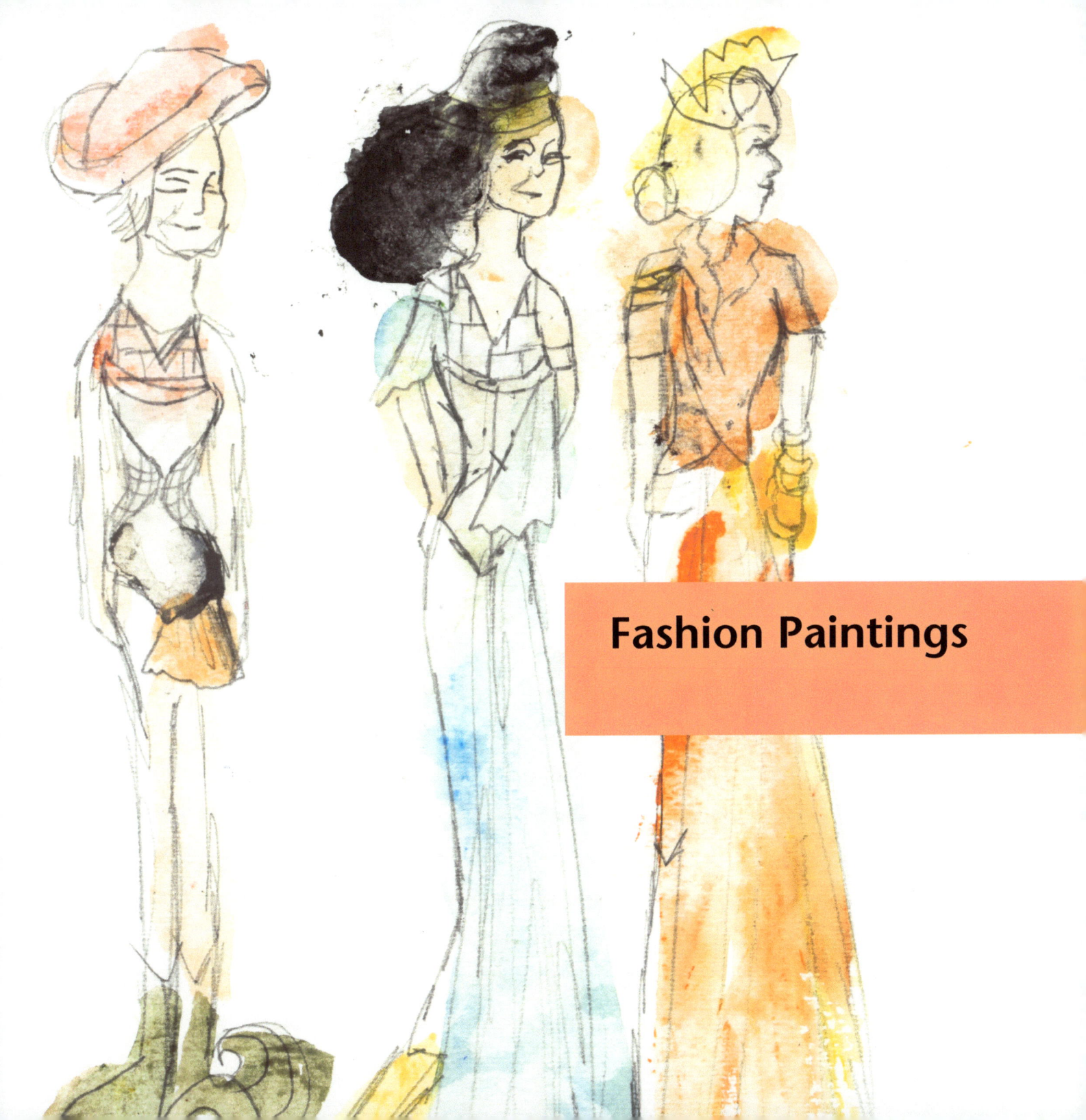

Fashion Paintings

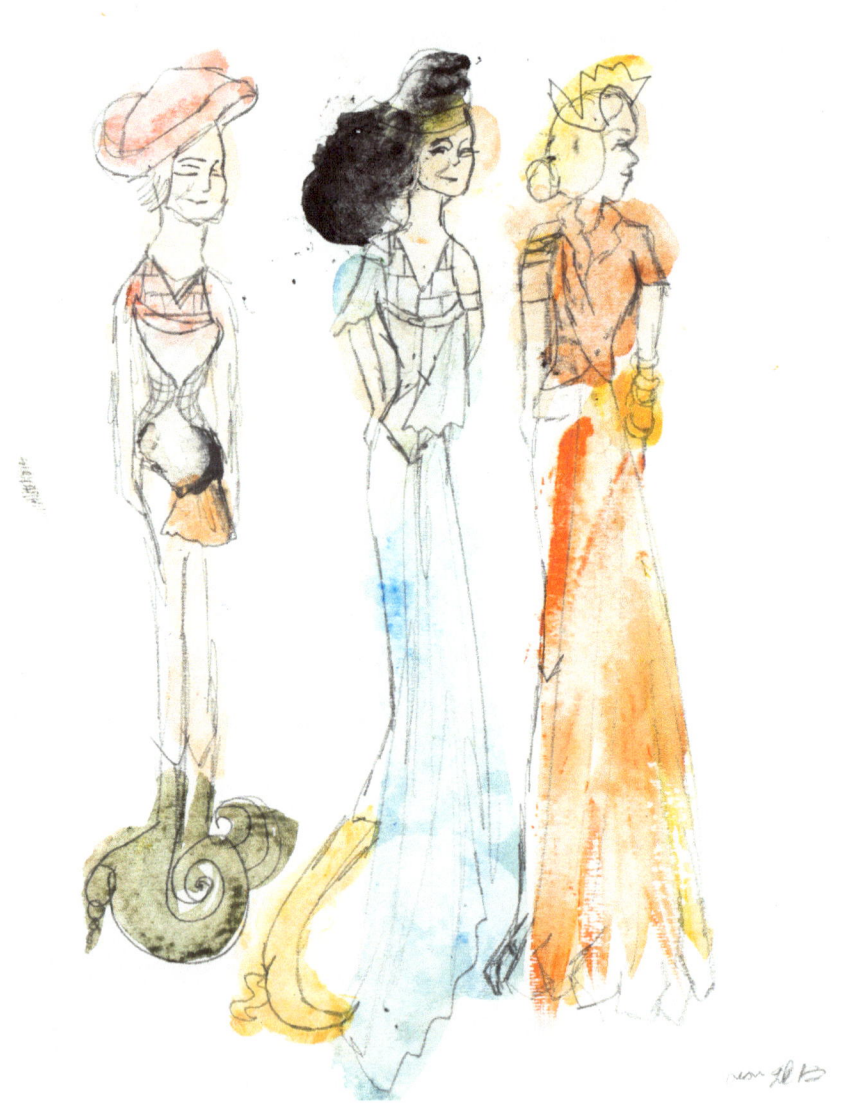

Lady Gaga Clothes
Watercolor and pencil on paper, 12 x 9 inches
2012
Courtesy of Nancy and Alan Hoffman

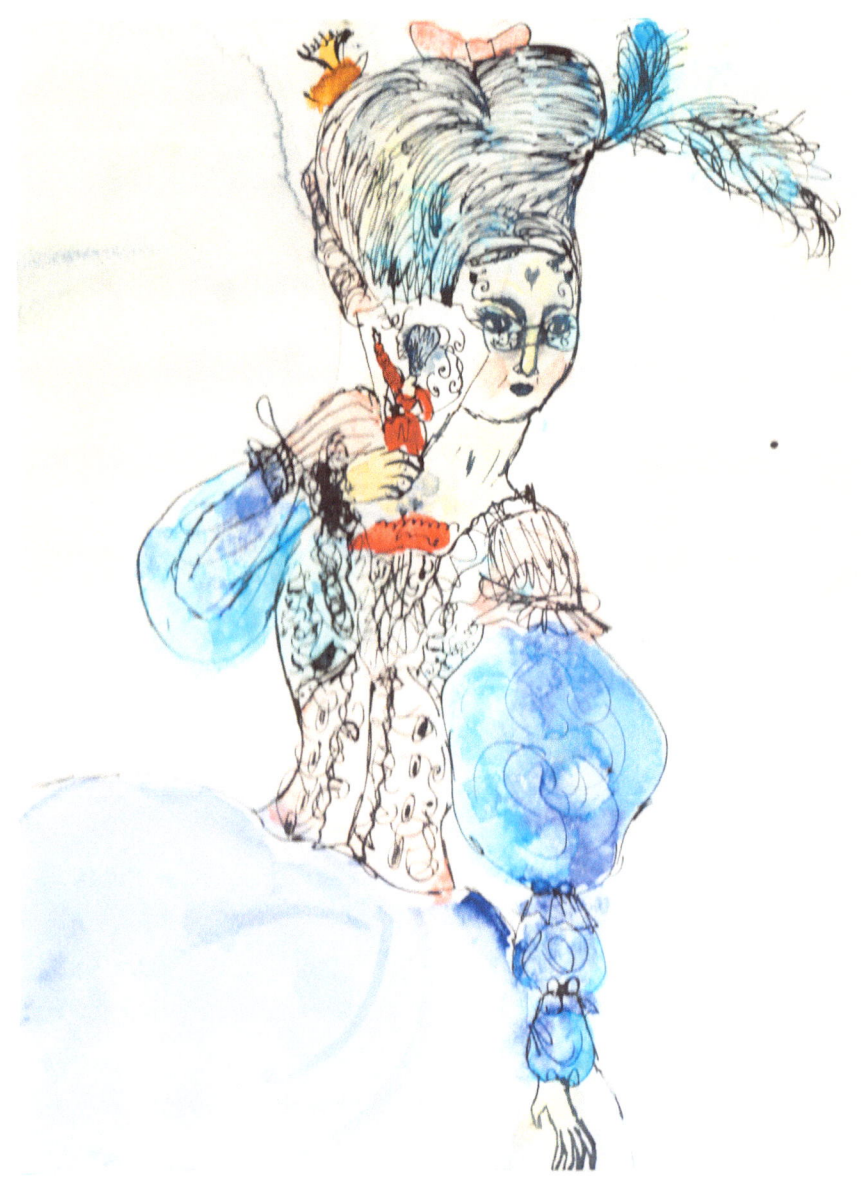

Carlotta (after Maira Kalman)
Watercolor and ink on paper, 11.5 x 8.5 inches
2012
Courtesy of Jessica and Laurence Sheinman

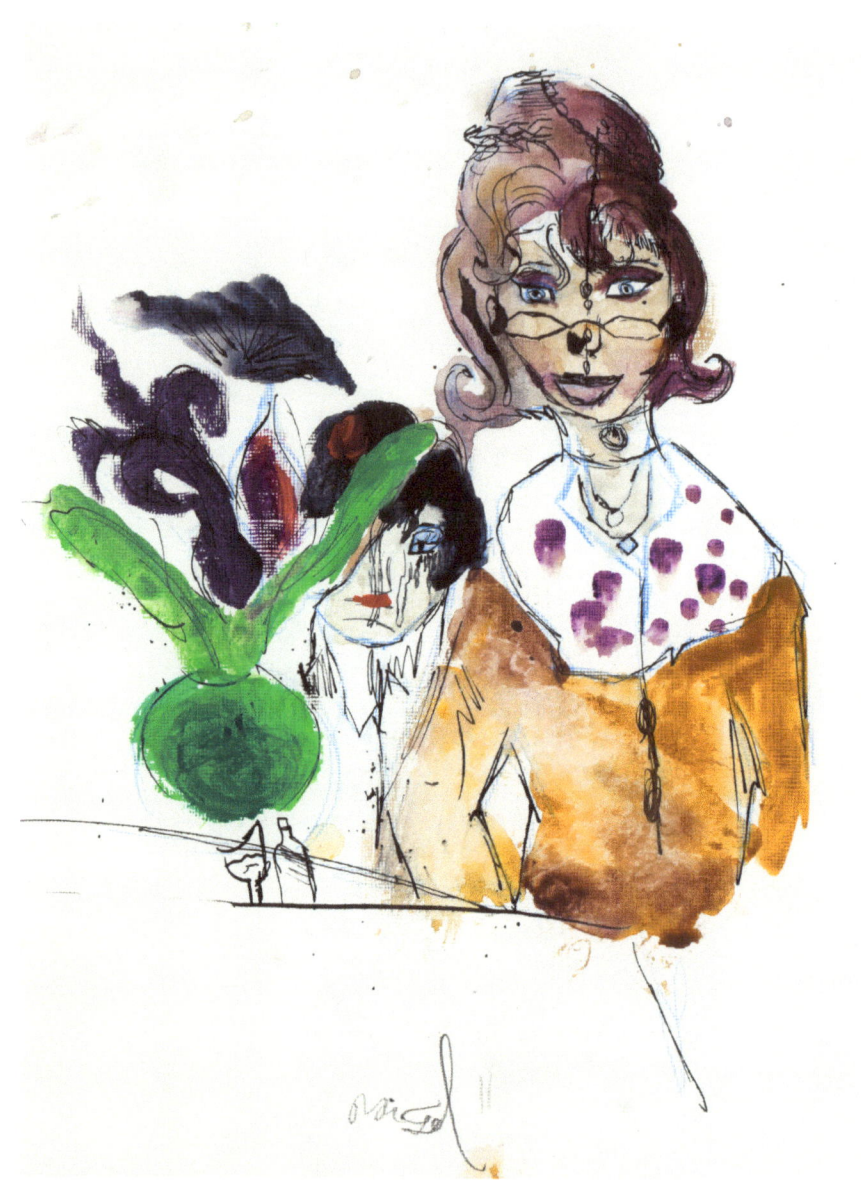

Talk Show
Watercolor and ink on paper, 12 x 9 inches
2011
Courtesy of Marcia and Naftali Tal

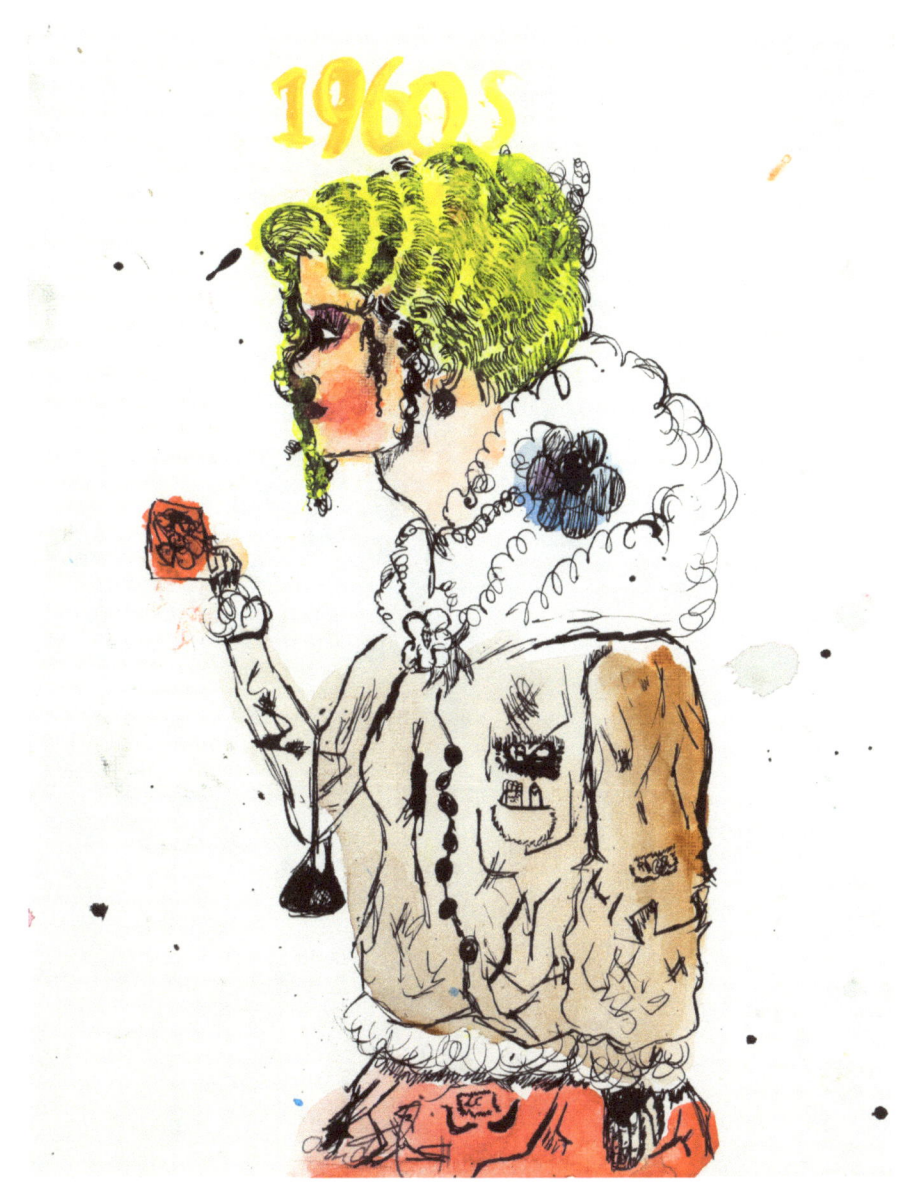

60's
Watercolor and ink on paper, 12 x 9 inches
2011
Courtesy of Efrat and Yaron Ziegel and family

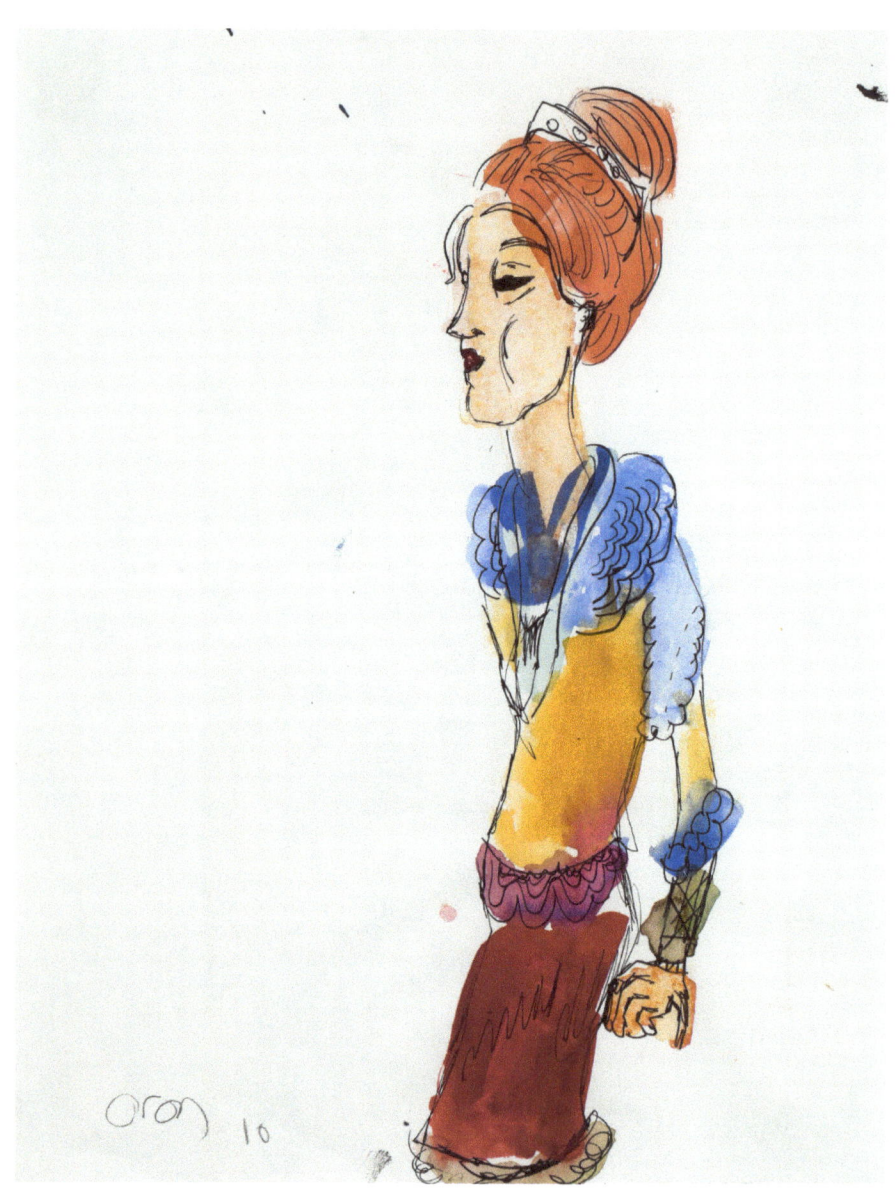

The Lady
Watercolor and ink on paper, 11.5 x 9 inches
2010
Courtesy of Dr. Karen and Mitchell Fleiss

Imagination (detail)

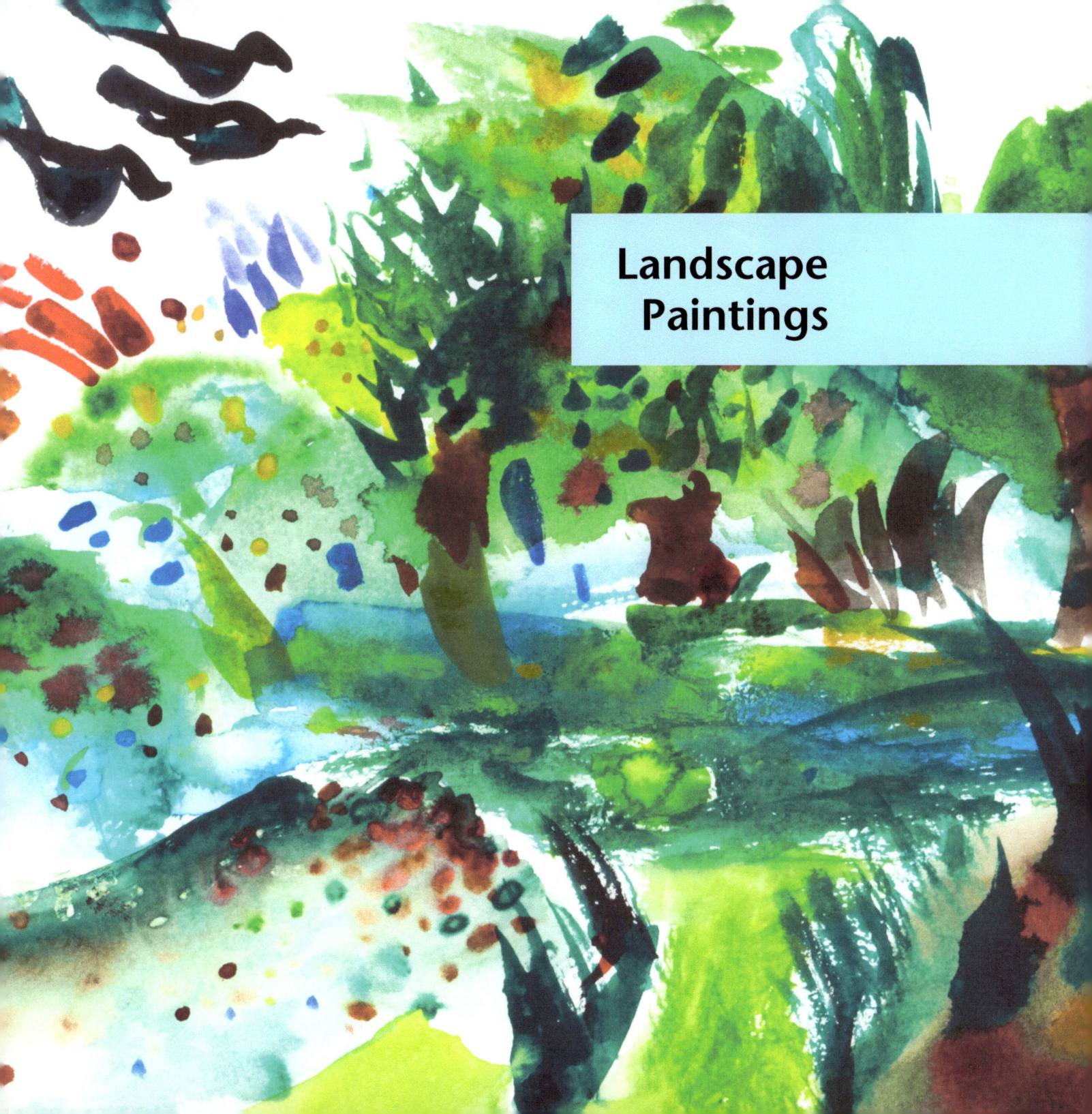

Landscape
Paintings

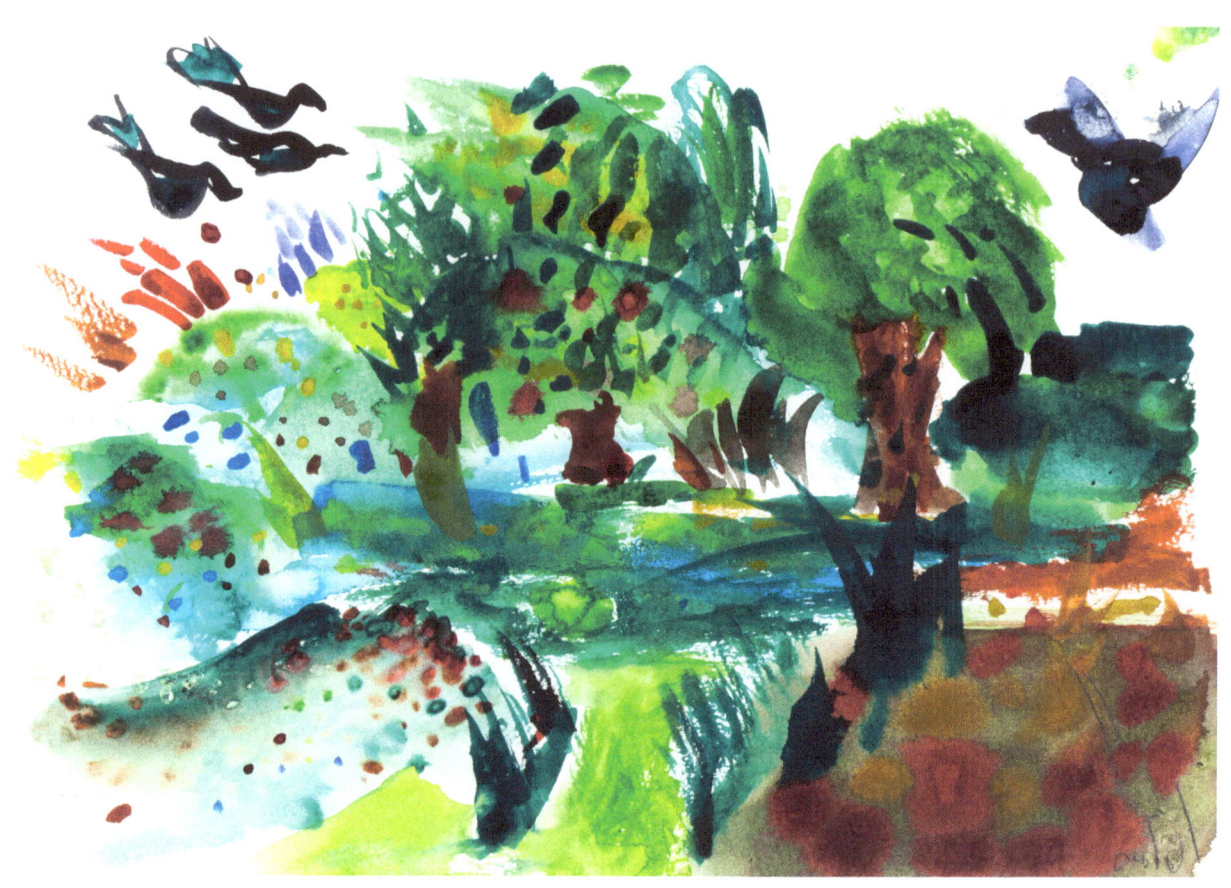

Imagination
Watercolor on paper, 6.25 x 9 inches
2011
Courtesy of Marcia and Naftali Tal

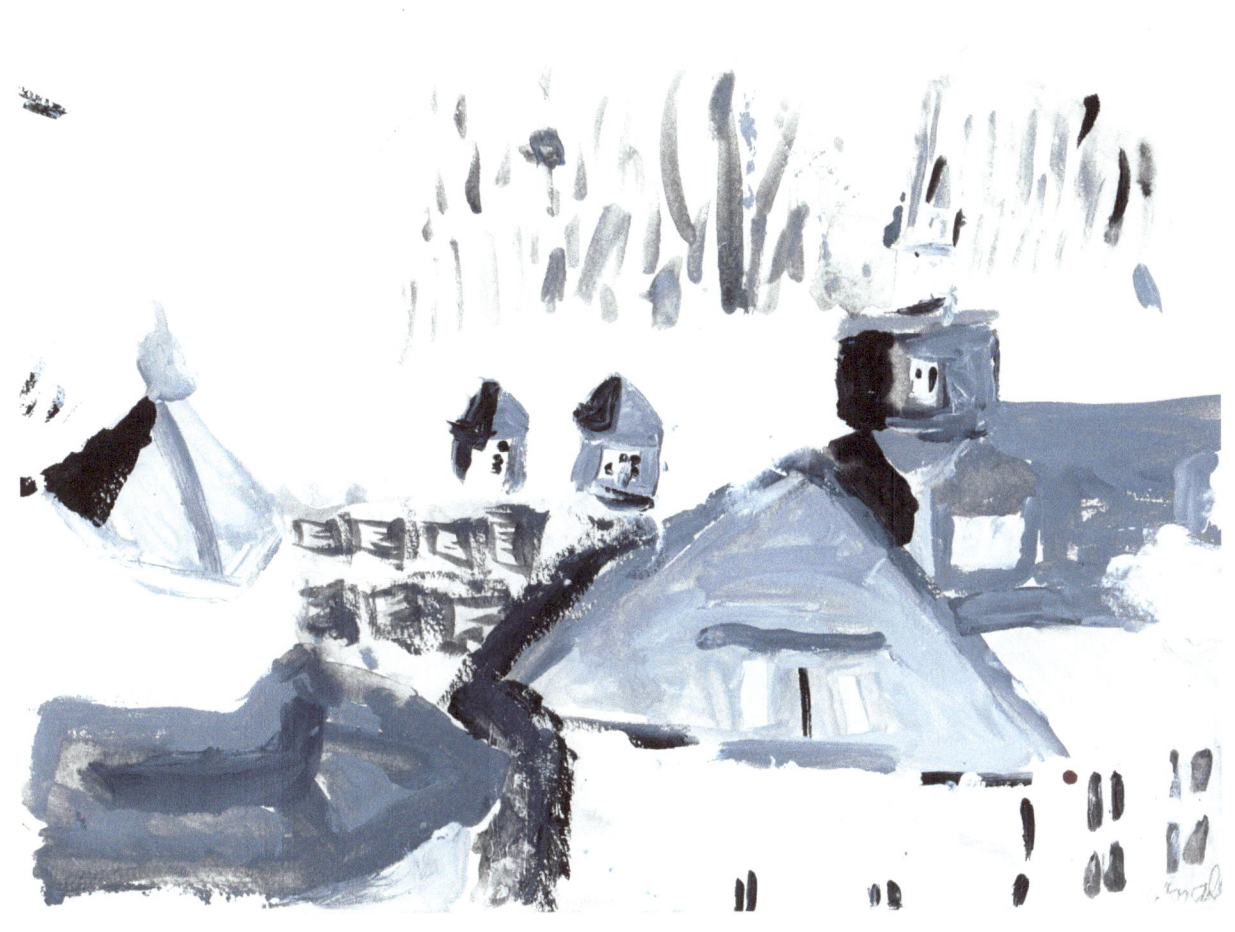

Tremblant (grayscale)
Acrylic on paper, 9 x 12 inches
2012
Courtesy of Naomi and Irwin Horowitz

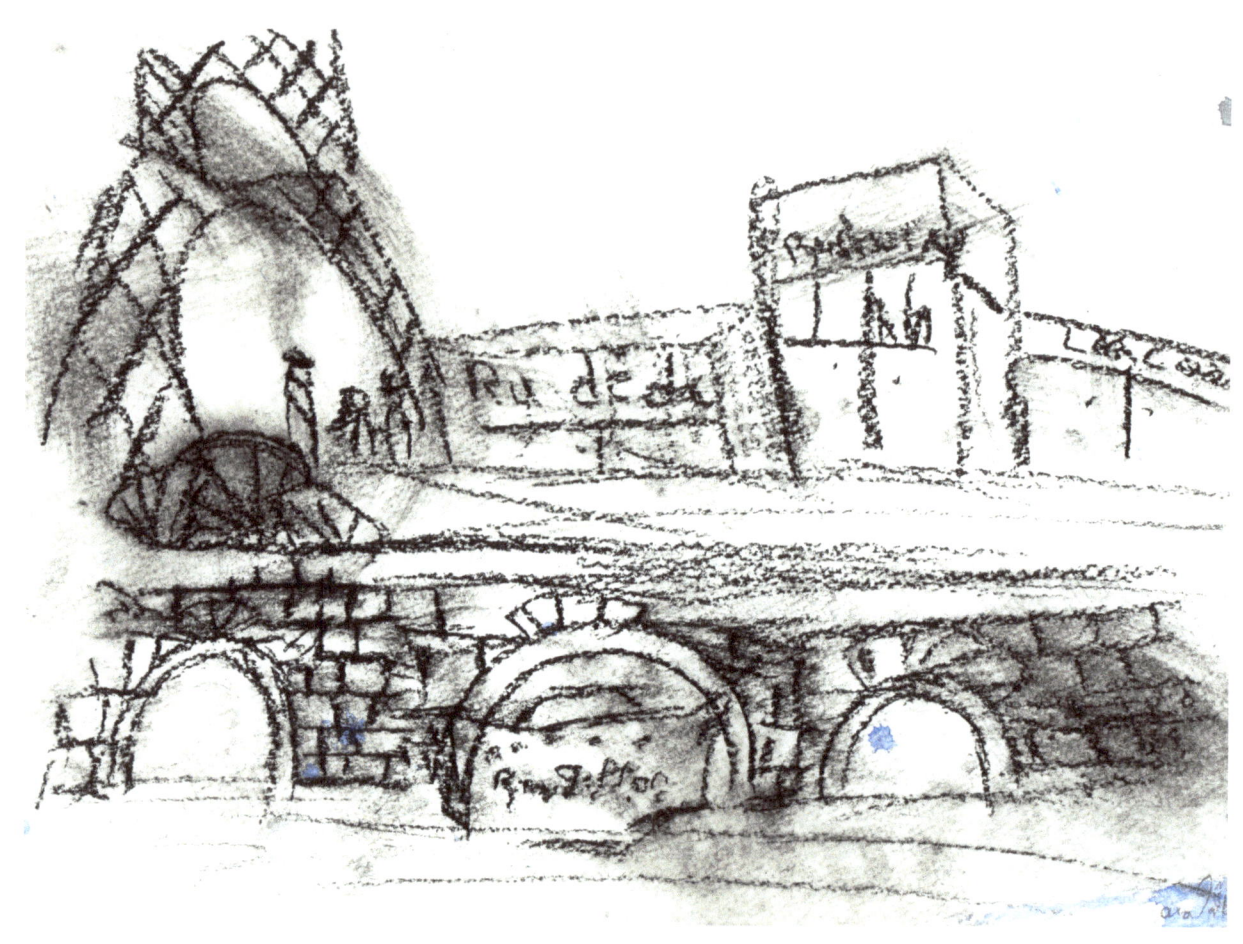

Paris-1939
Conté crayon on paper, 9 x 12 inches
2012
Courtesy of Irma and Steve Wilk

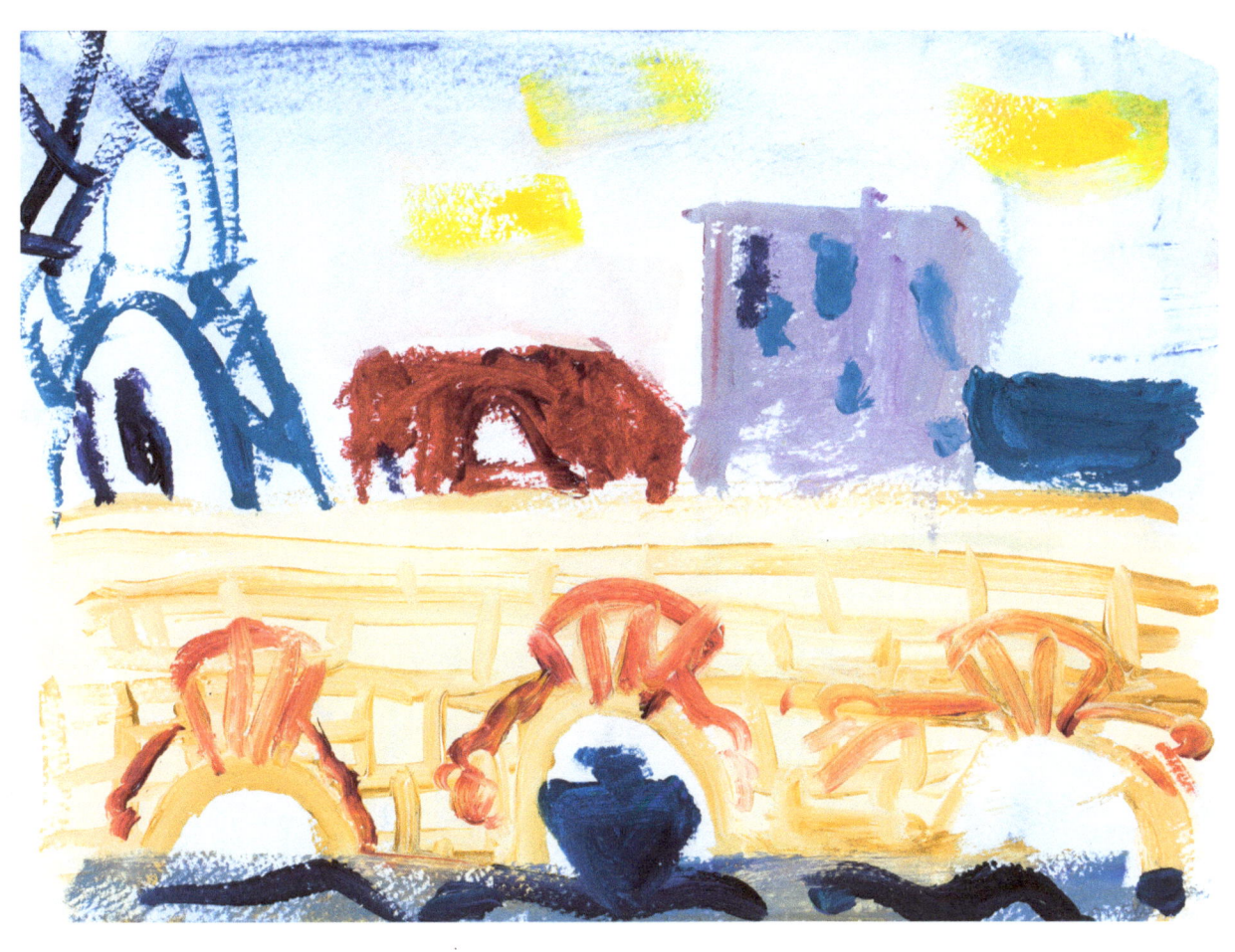

Paris-1992
Acrylic on paper, 9 x 12 inches
2012
Courtesy of Michael Seidenfeld

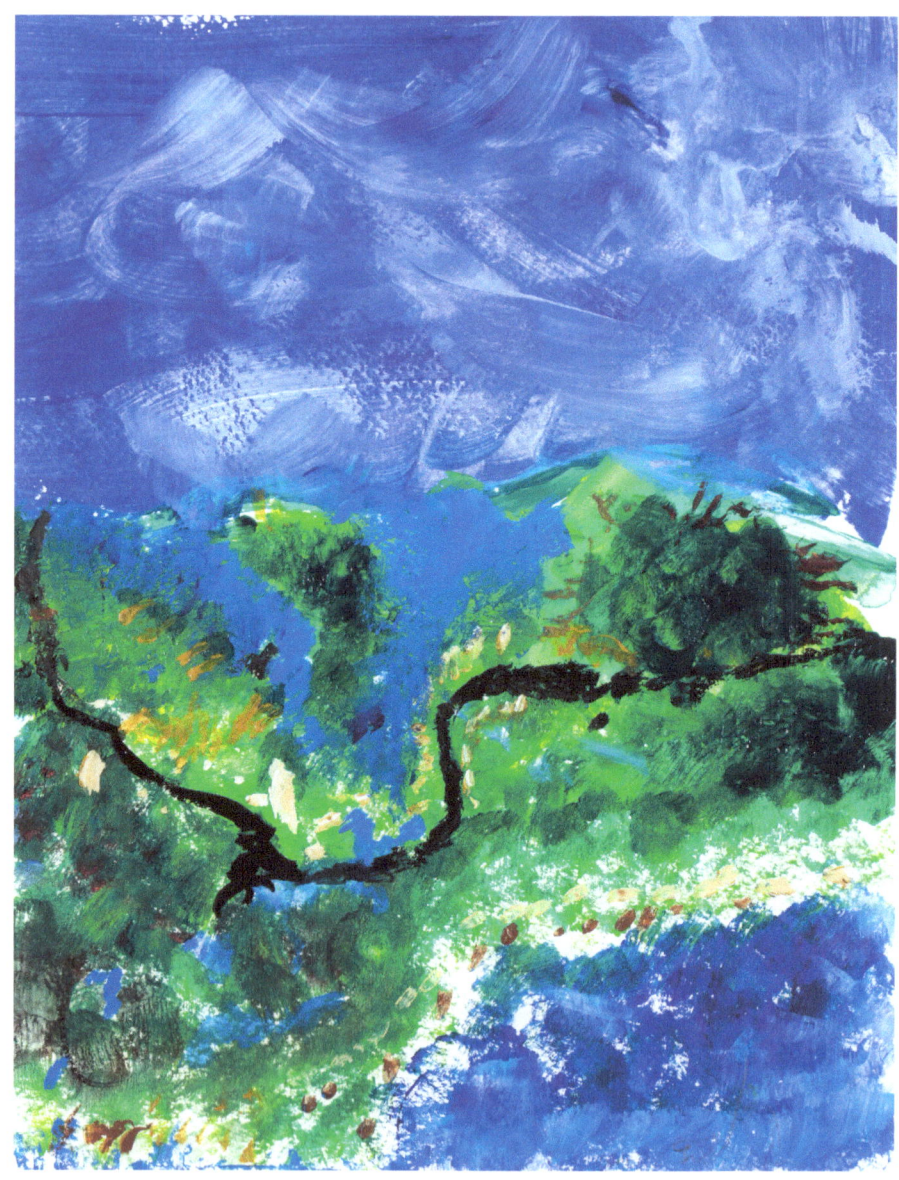

French Landscape with Additional Countries
Acrylic on paper, 9 x 11.5 inches
2011
Courtesy of Steven Seidenfeld

Cat, cat cat.....yarn (detail)

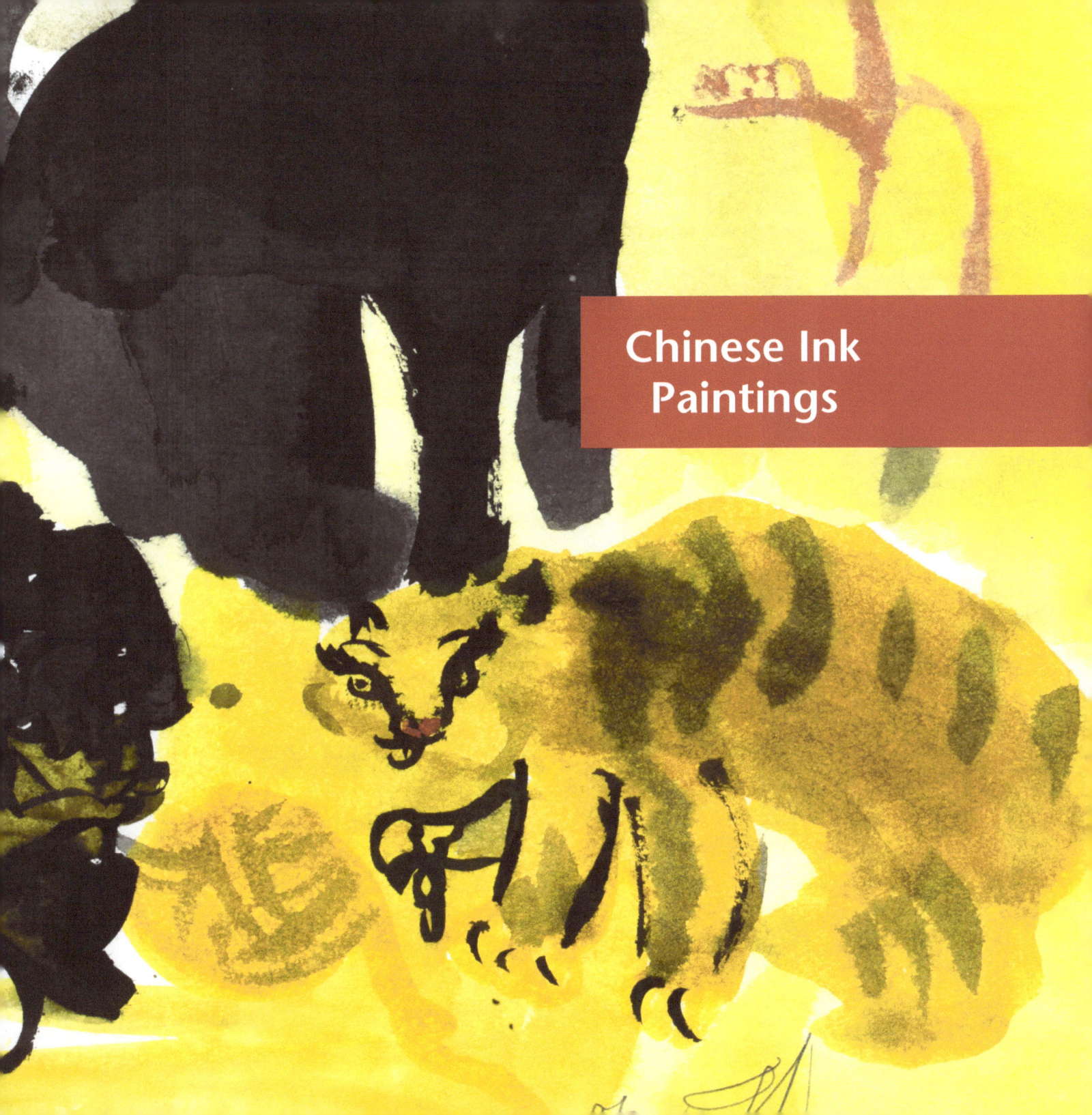

Chinese Ink
Paintings

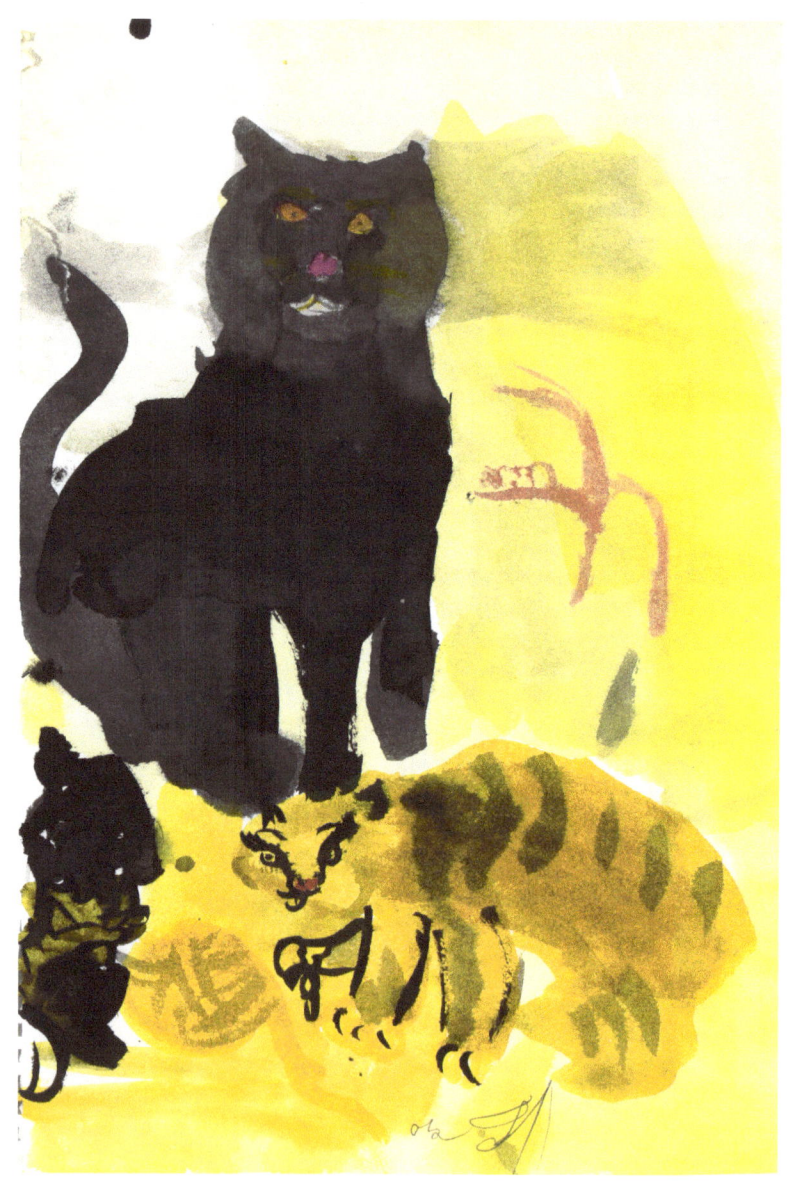

Cat, cat cat.....yarn
Ink on paper, 15 x 9.5 inches
2011
Courtesy of Rabbi David Wise and Judy Krinitz and family

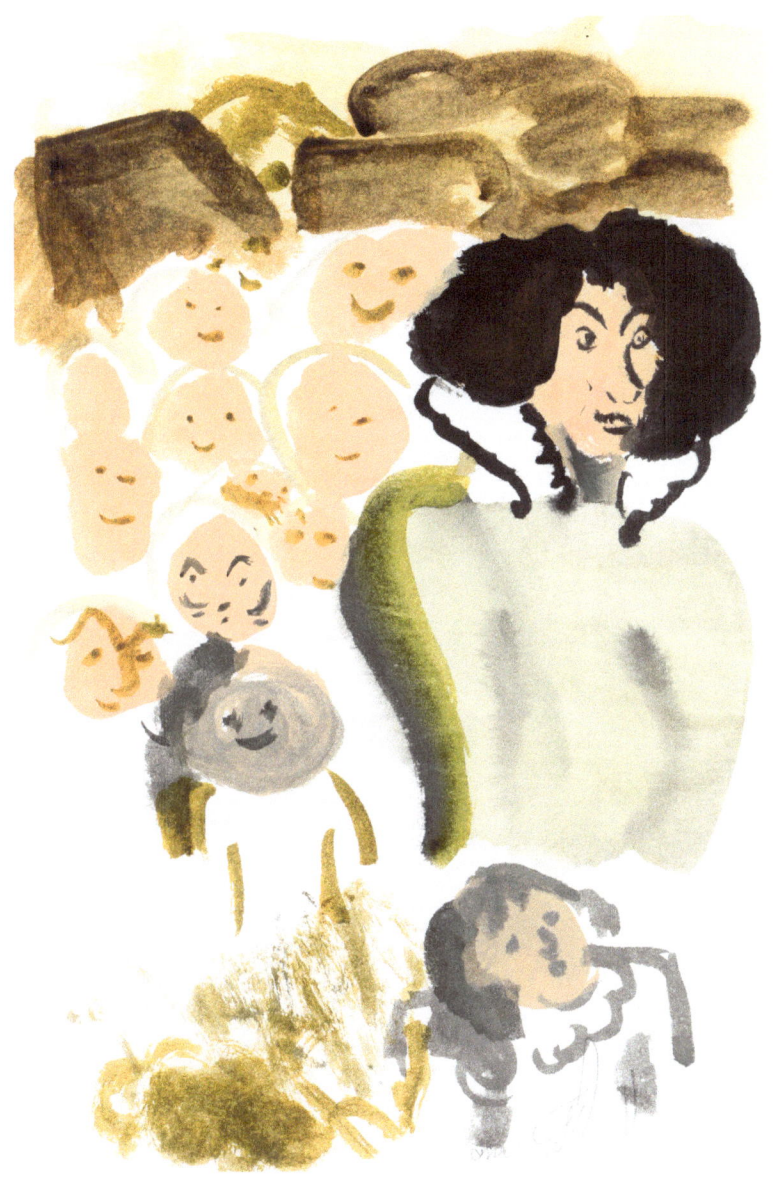

Parade
Watercolor, ink and acrylic on paper, 15 x 9.5 inches
2011
Courtesy of Laurie and David Kalman

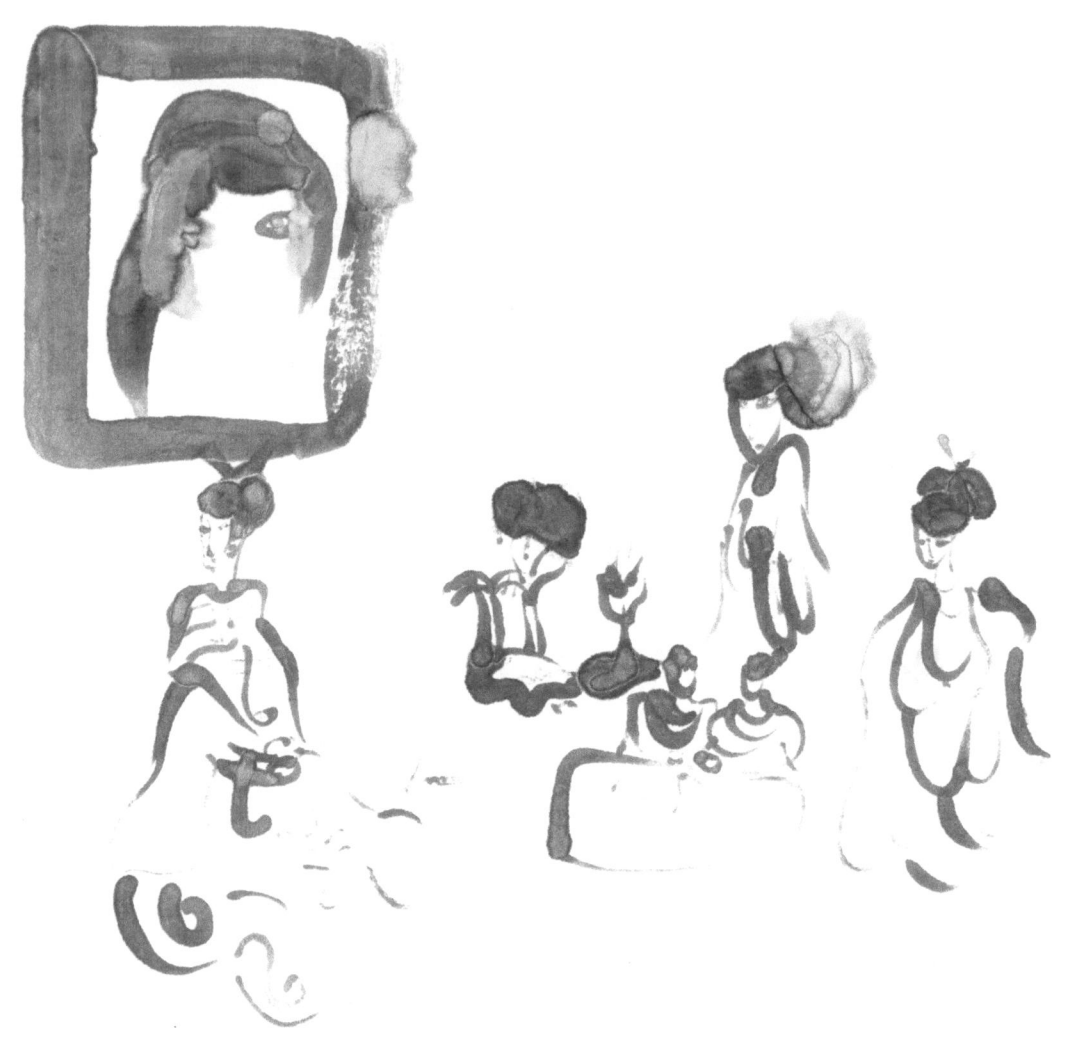

Untitled
Ink on Chinese paper, 15 x 16 inches
2012
Courtesy of Abigail Ward

Le Chandelier (detail)

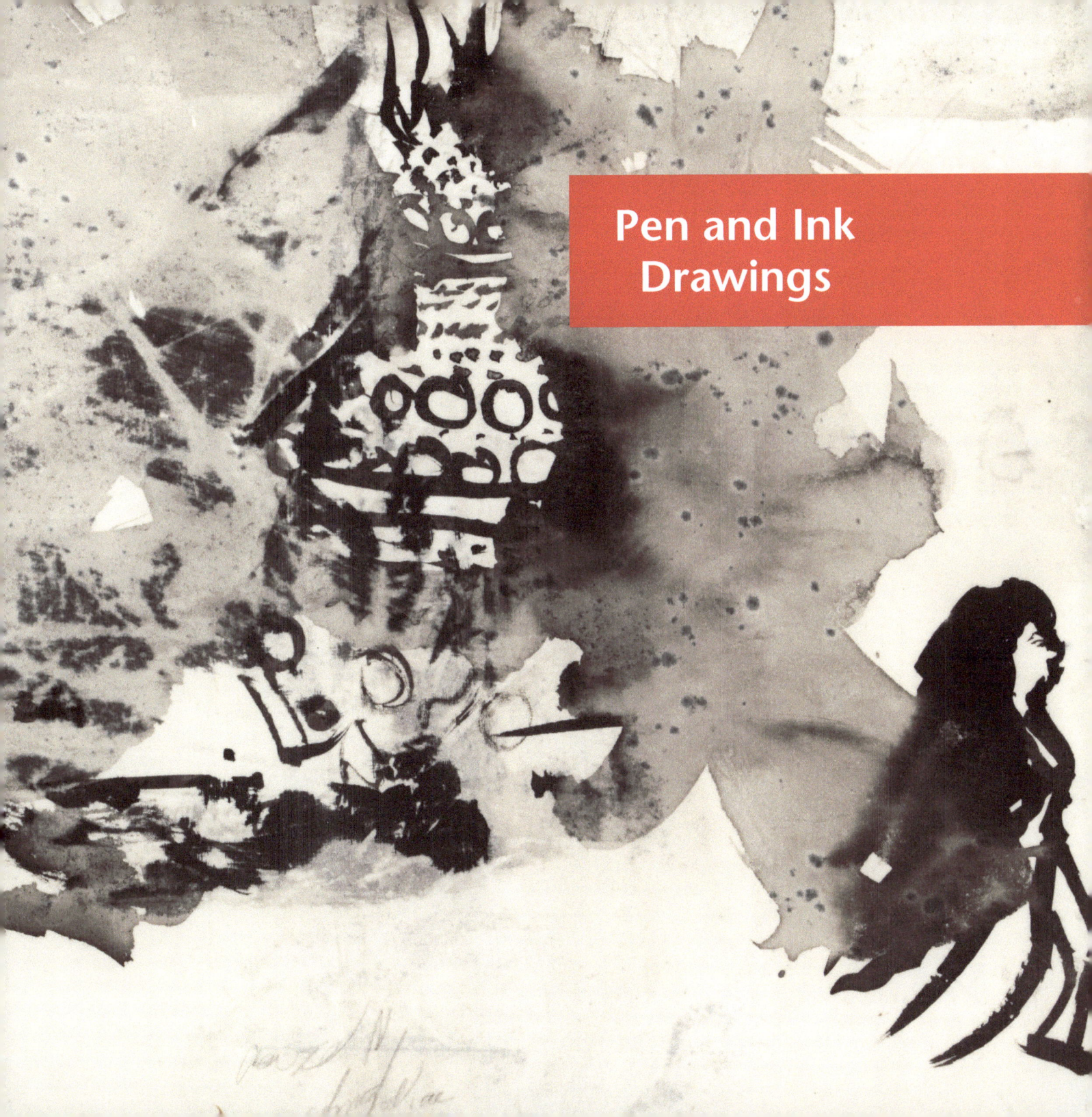

Pen and Ink Drawings

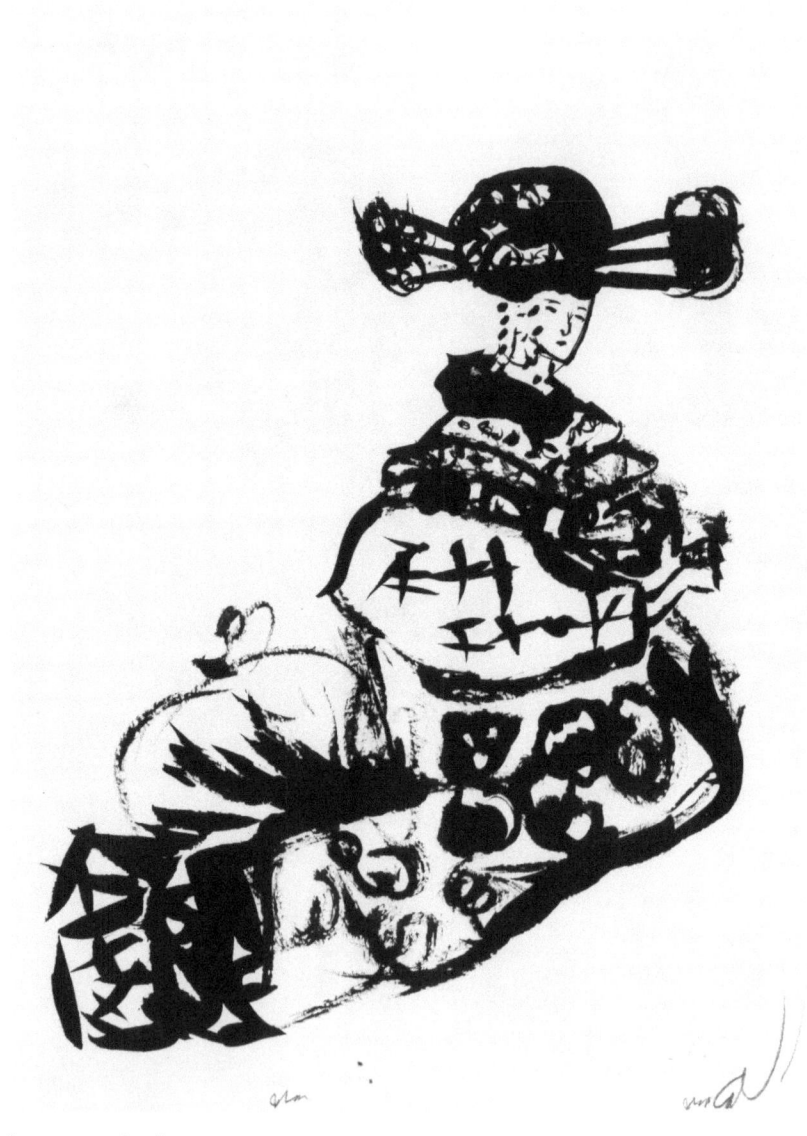

Japanese Lady
Ink on paper, 9 x 6.25 inches
2011
Courtesy of Marie Rego

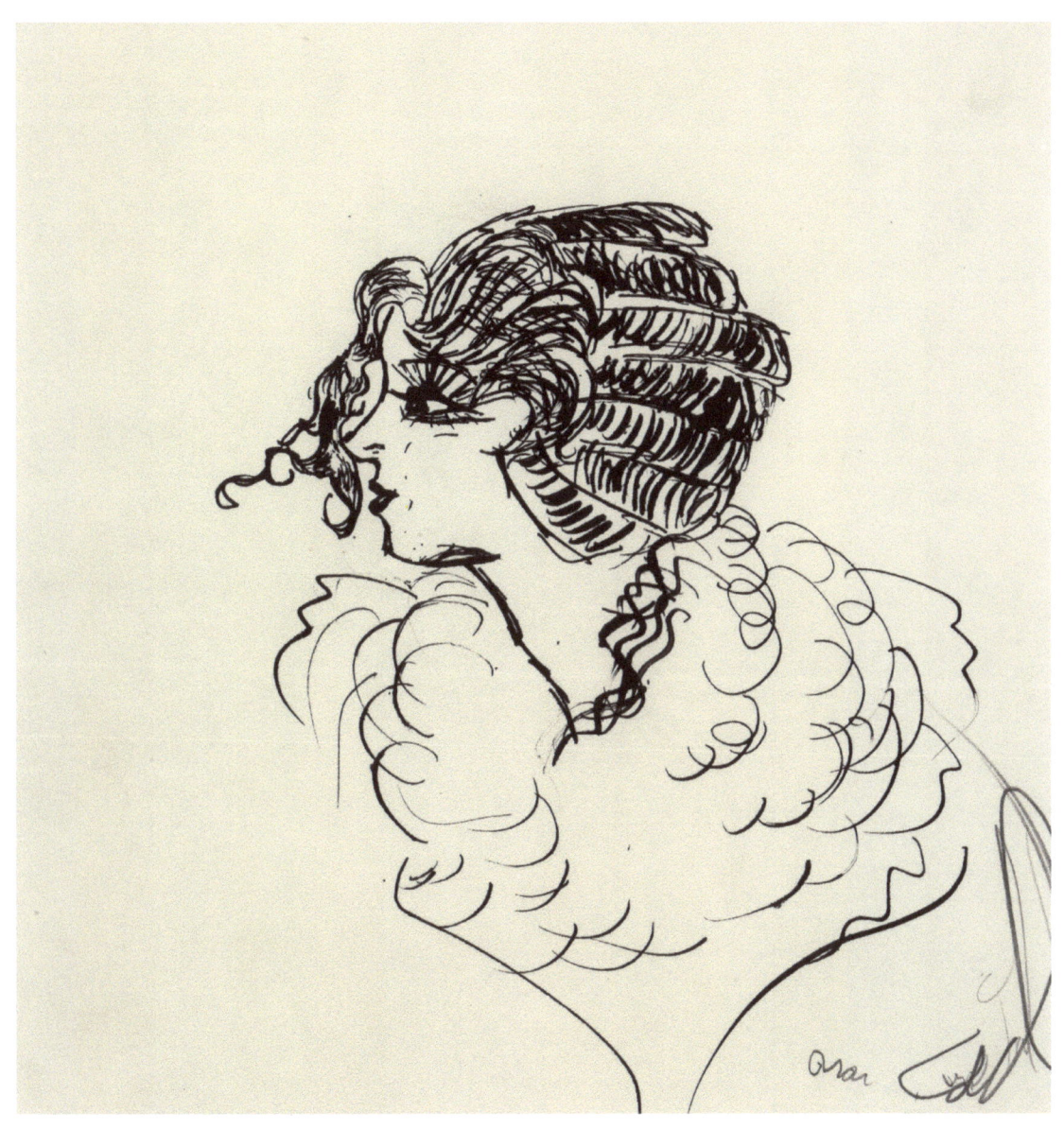

Untitled
Ink on paper, 7 x 6.5 inches
2011

Courtesy of Lynn and Natan Gonen

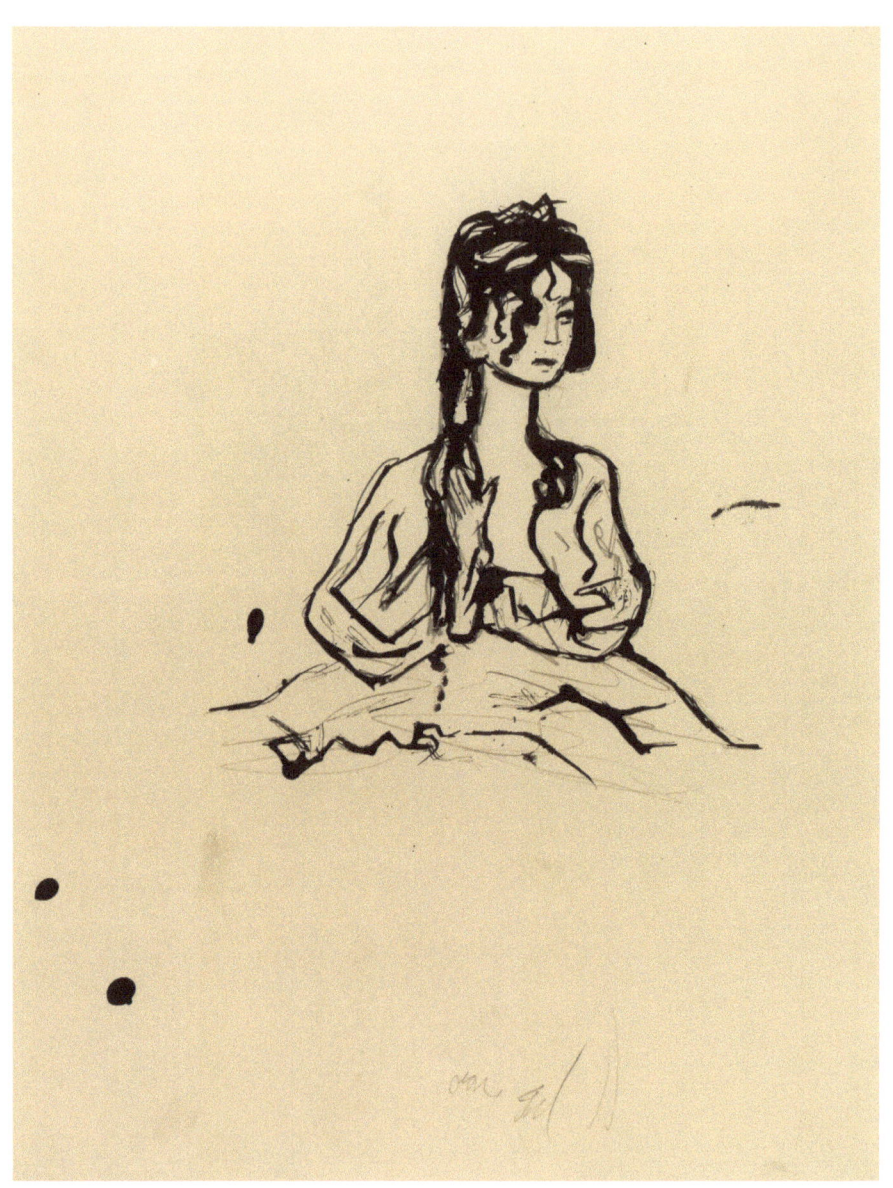

Lady in Water
Ink on paper, 7.5 x 6.75 inches
2011
Courtesy of Sherry and Barry Simon

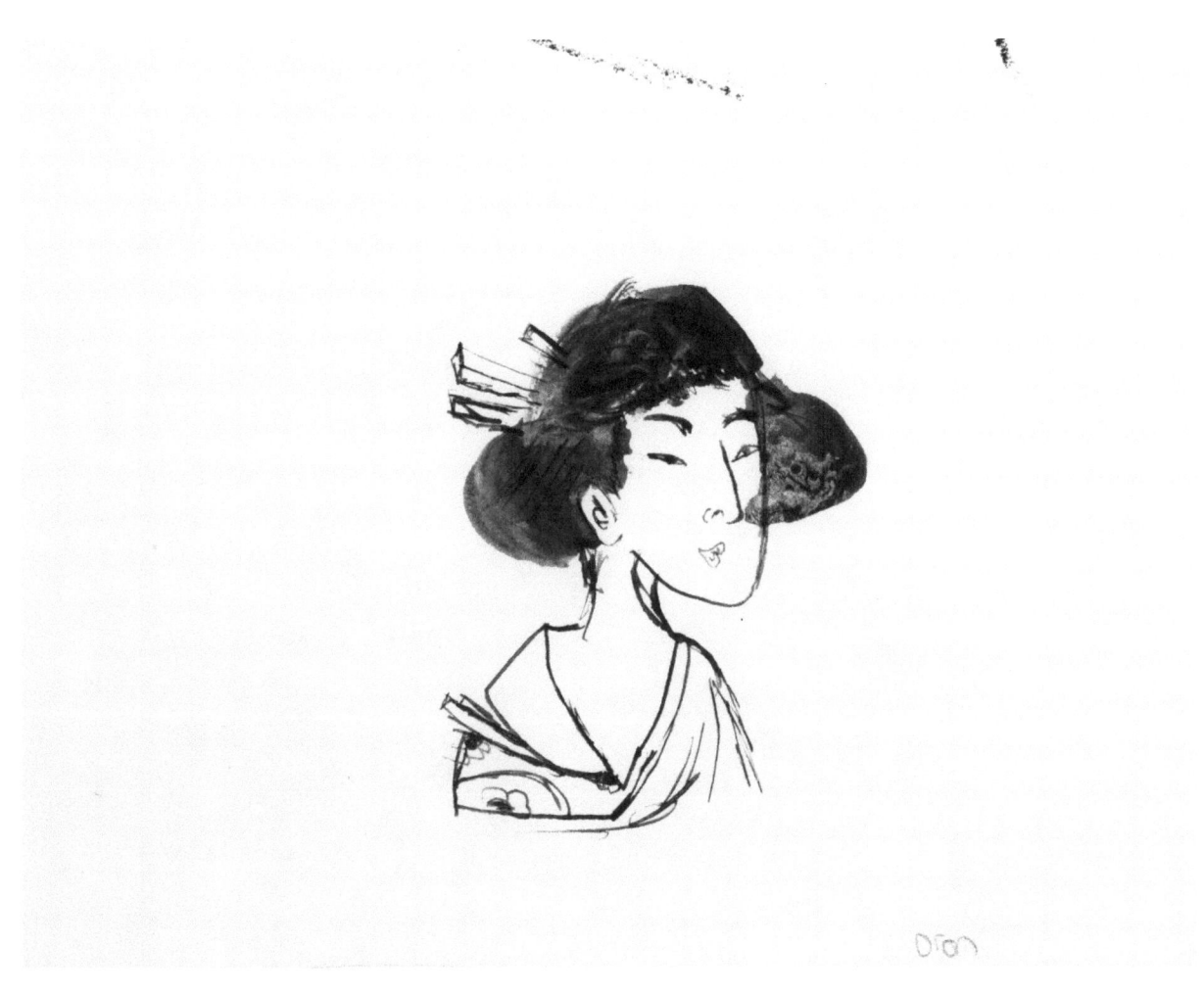

Untitled
Ink on paper, 6 x 7.5 inches
2010
Courtesy of Oron Tal

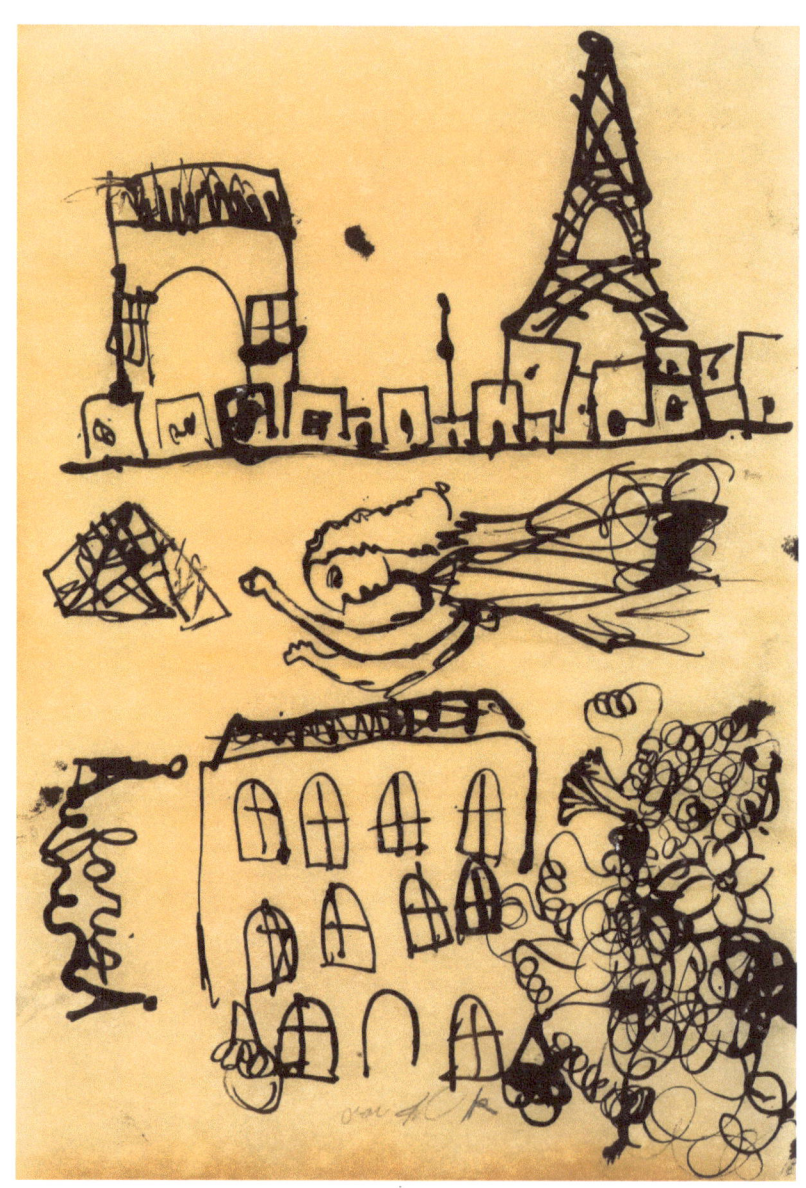

Paris
Ink on vellum, 10 x 7 inches
2012
Courtesy of Juan Gabriel c. Zorrilla

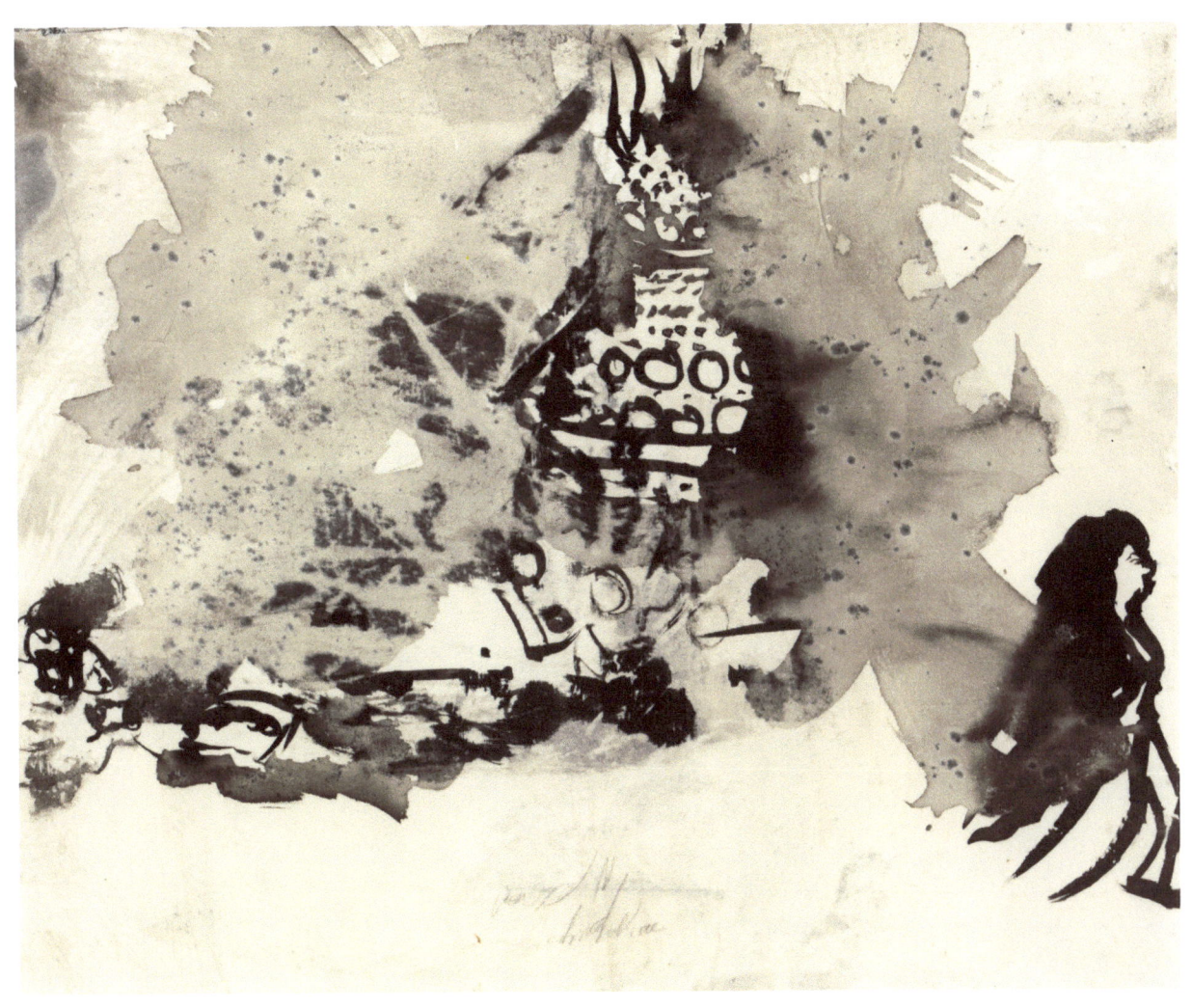

Le Chandelier
Ink on silk, 9.25 x 11 inches
2011
Courtesy of Marla and Jorge Cornejo

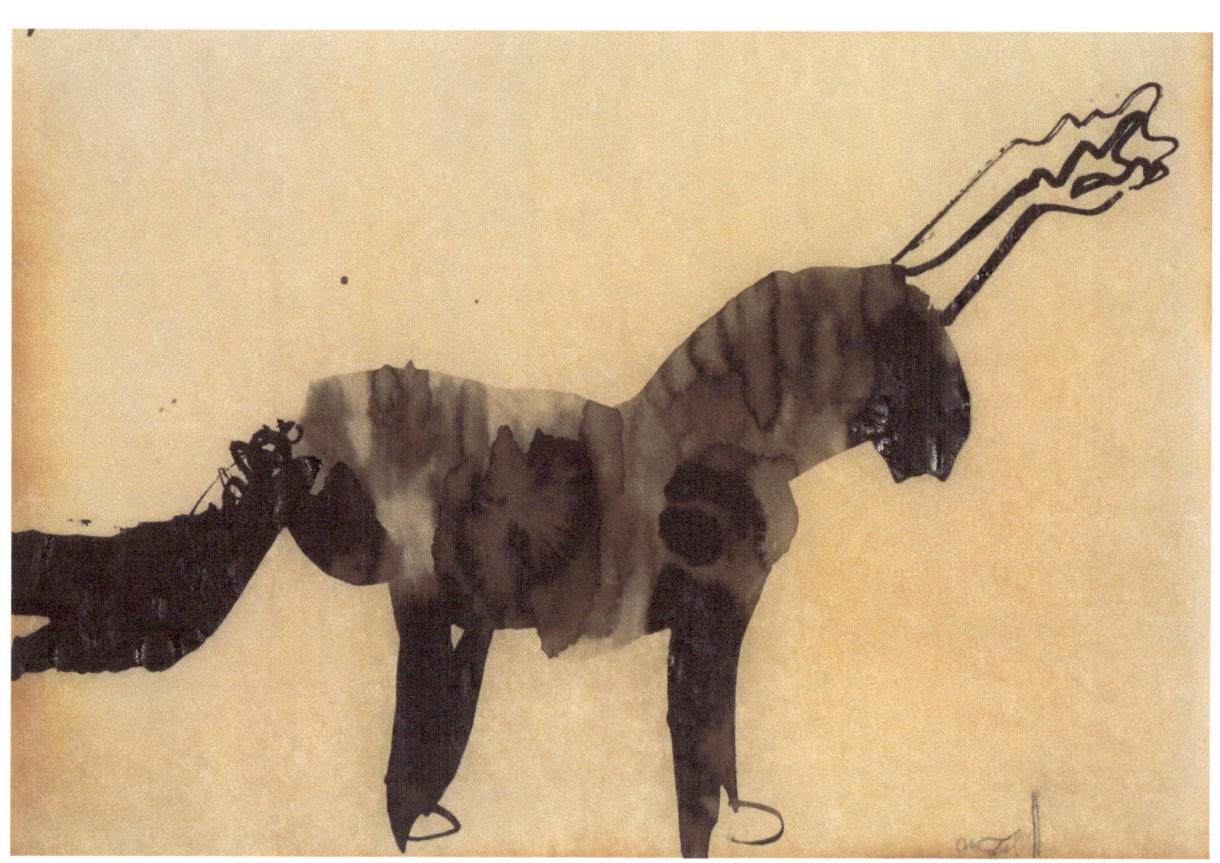

Untitled
Ink on vellum, 7 x 10 inches
2011
Courtesy of Valentina DuBasky

62 |

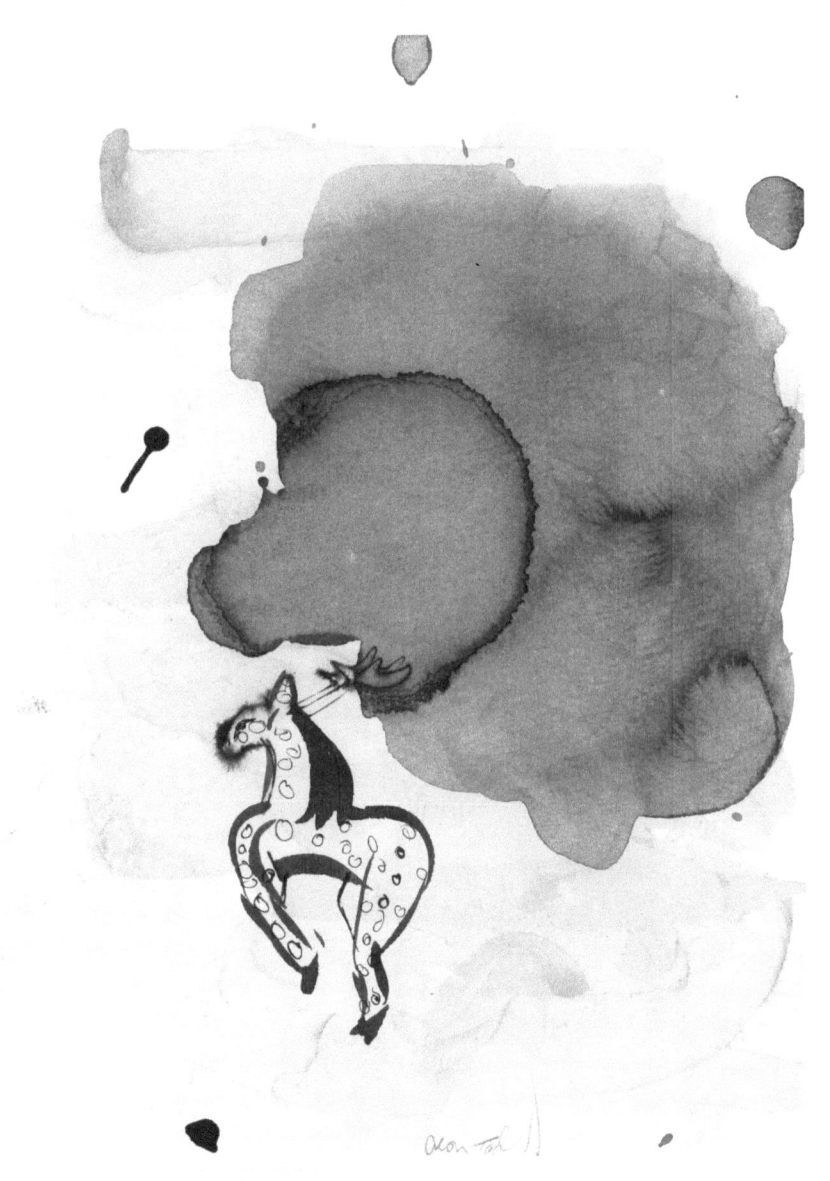

The Deer and the Cloud
Ink on paper, 9 x 6.25 inches
2011
Courtesy of Michelle Arrowood

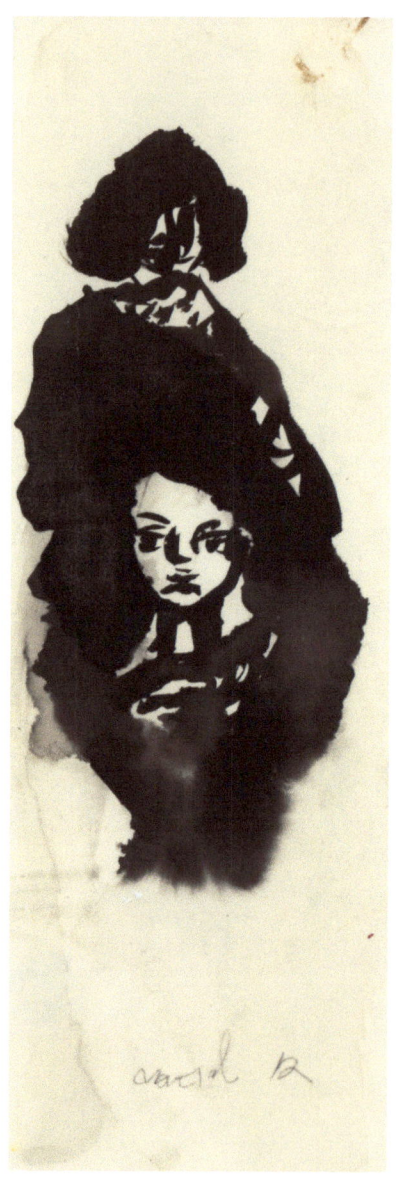

Moody People
Ink on silk, 12 x 4 inches
2012
Courtesy of Marjorie and Martin Mayerson

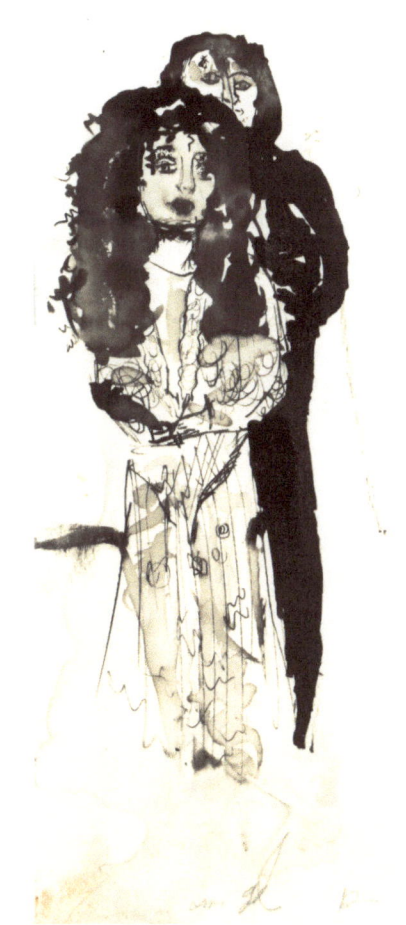

Phantom of the Opera Cellar
Ink on silk, 12 x 3.75 inches
2012
Courtesy of Eithan David

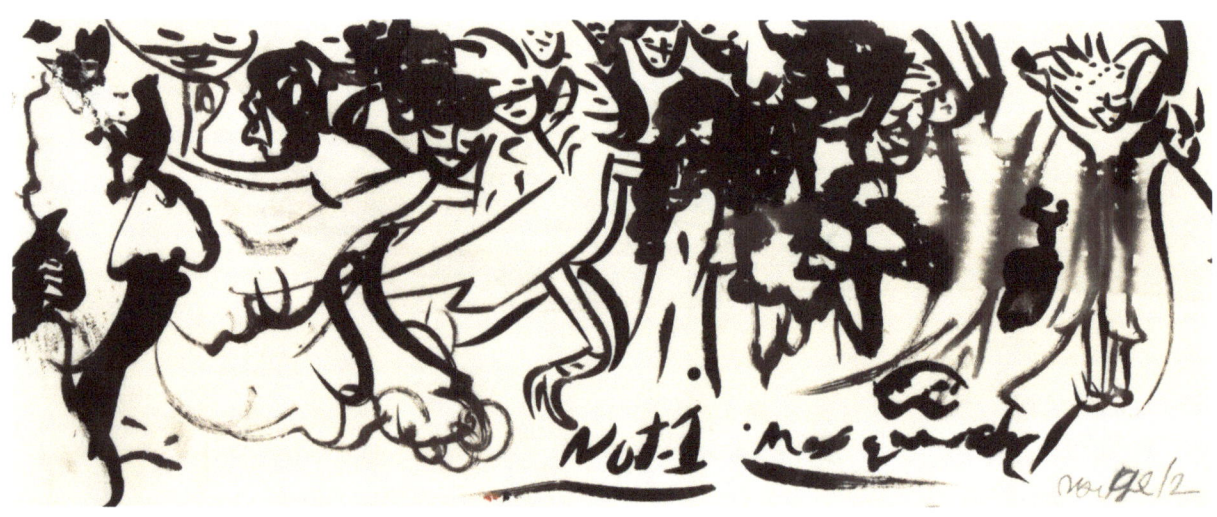

Masquerade
Ink on silk, 10 x 4 inches
2012
Courtesy of Adit Tal

Untitled II (detail)

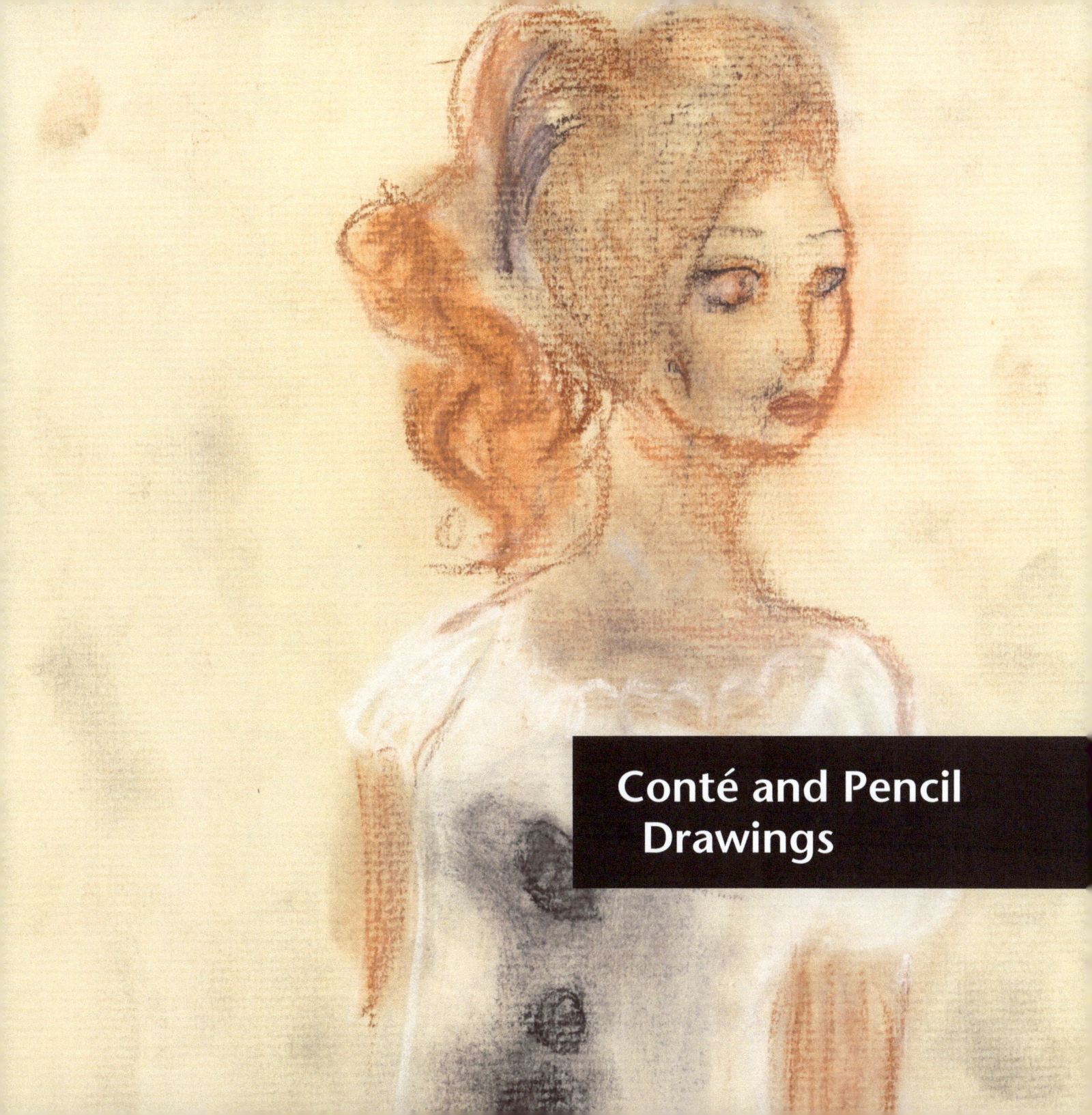

**Conté and Pencil
Drawings**

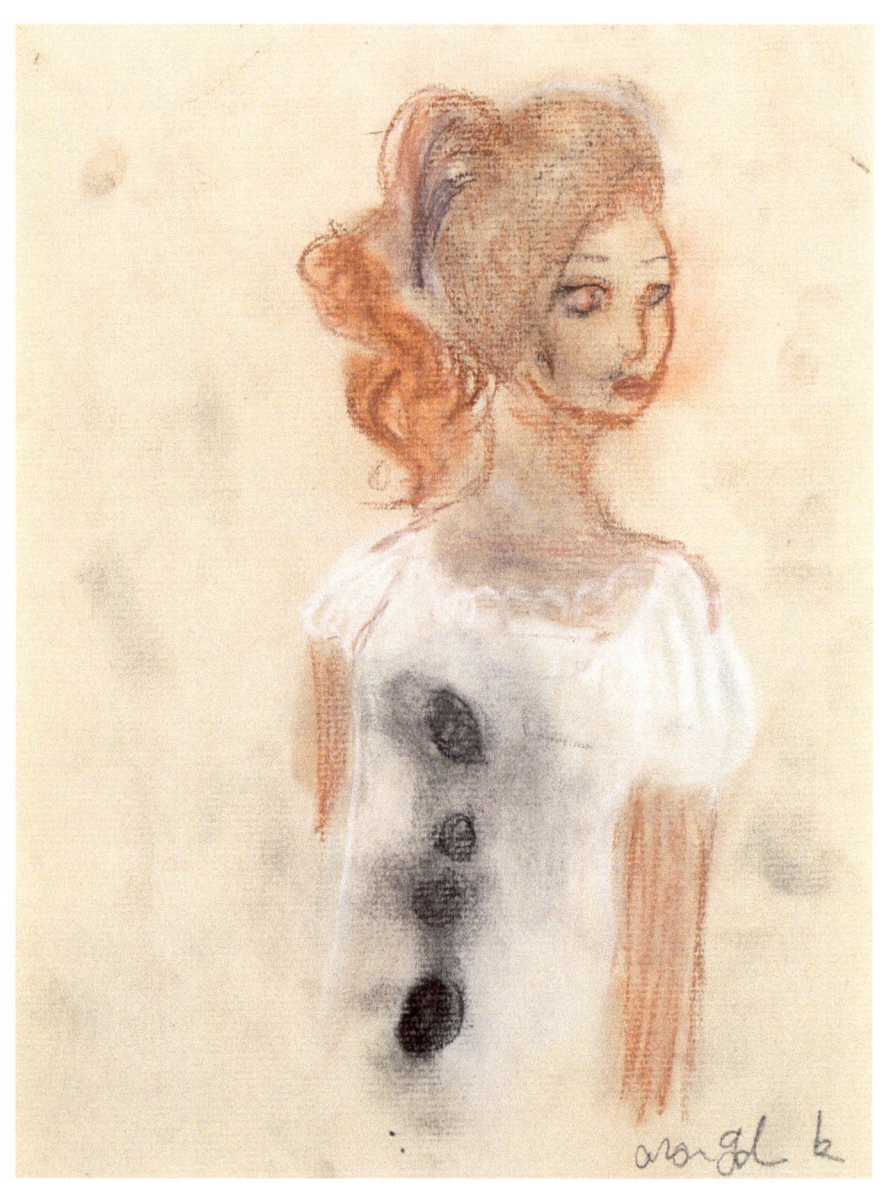

Untitled II
Conté crayon on paper, 8.25 x 6 inches
2012
Courtesy of Shelley and Ruvan Cohen

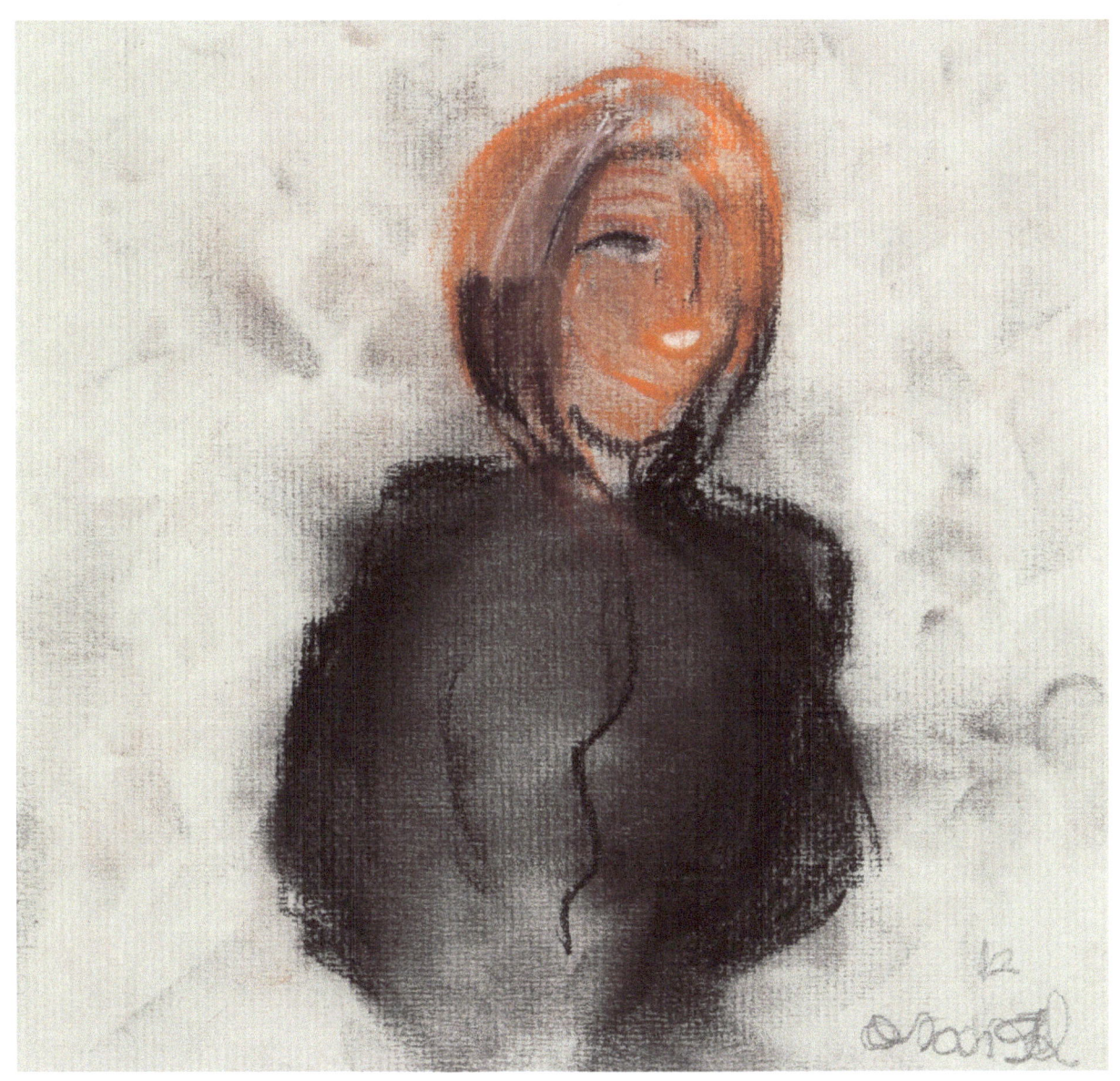

Untitled I
Conté crayon on paper, 6 x 6 inches
2012
Courtesy of Sherry and Barry Simon

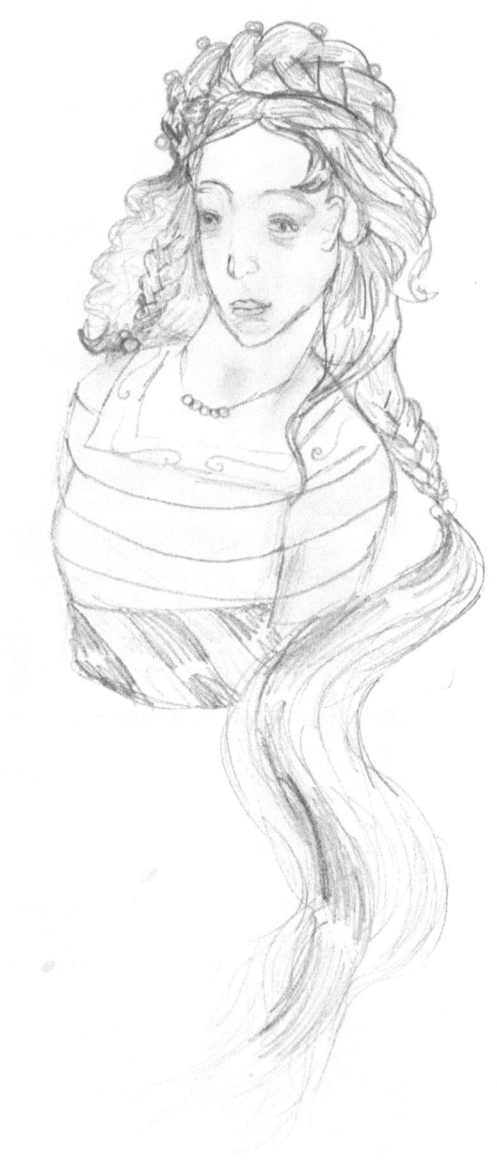

Untitled-Ufizzi I (after Sandro Botticelli)
Pencil on paper, 10.5 x 8 inches
2012
Courtesy of Karen and Ira Chazan

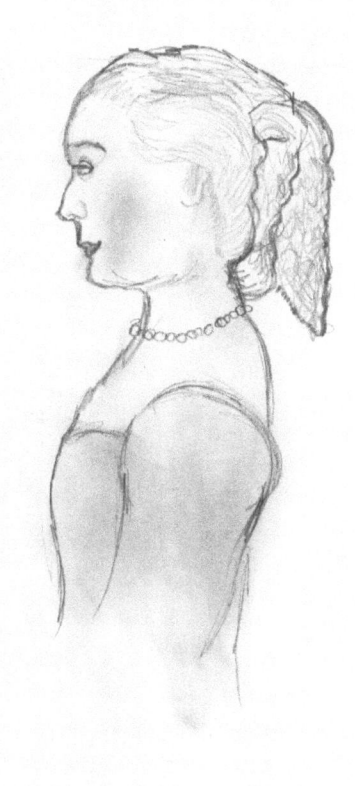

Untitled-Ufizzi II (after Sandro Botticelli)
Pencil on paper, 10.5 x 8 inches
2012
Courtesy of Karen and Ira Chazan

Oron Tal's Dream House (detail)

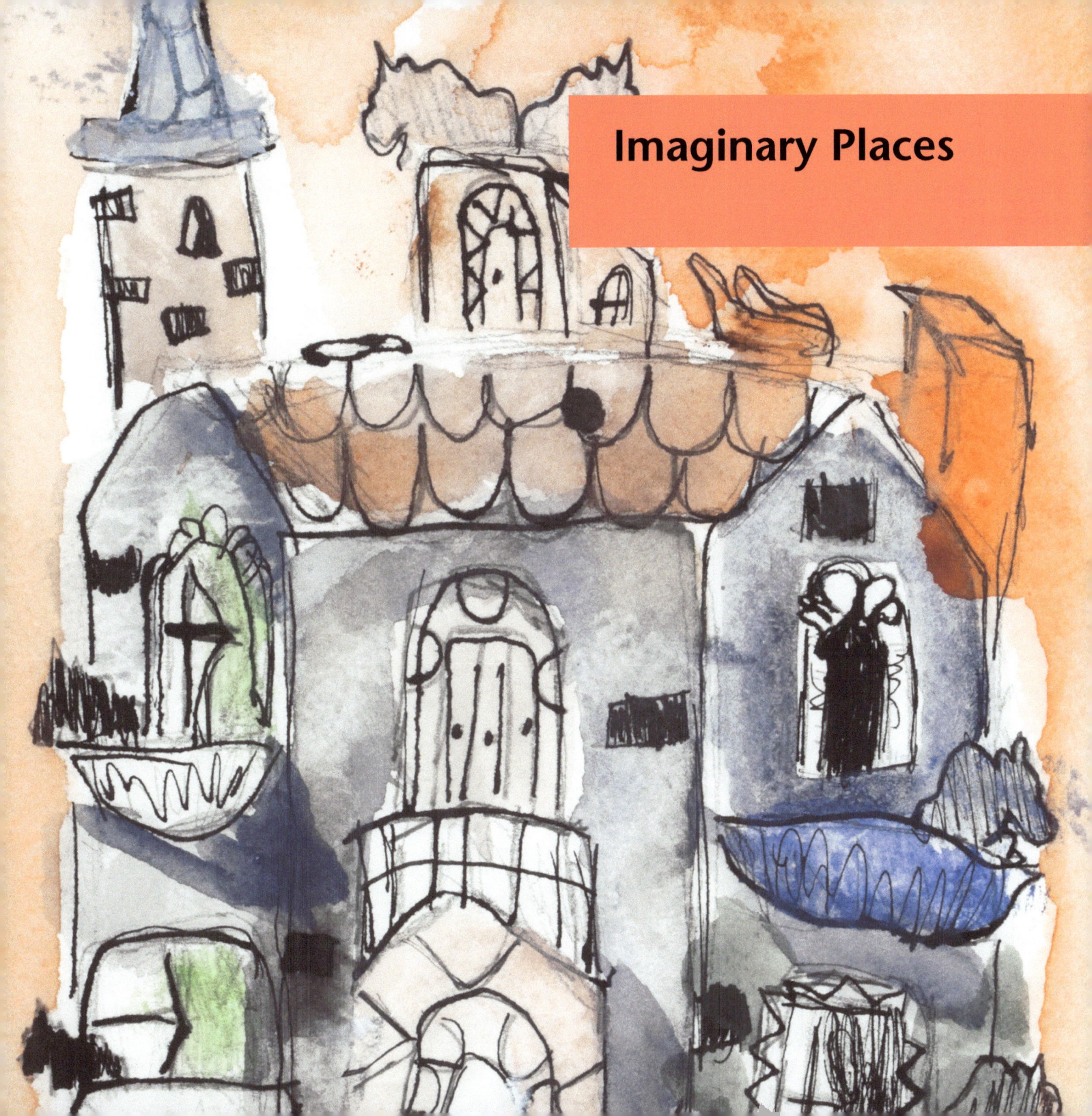

Imaginary Places

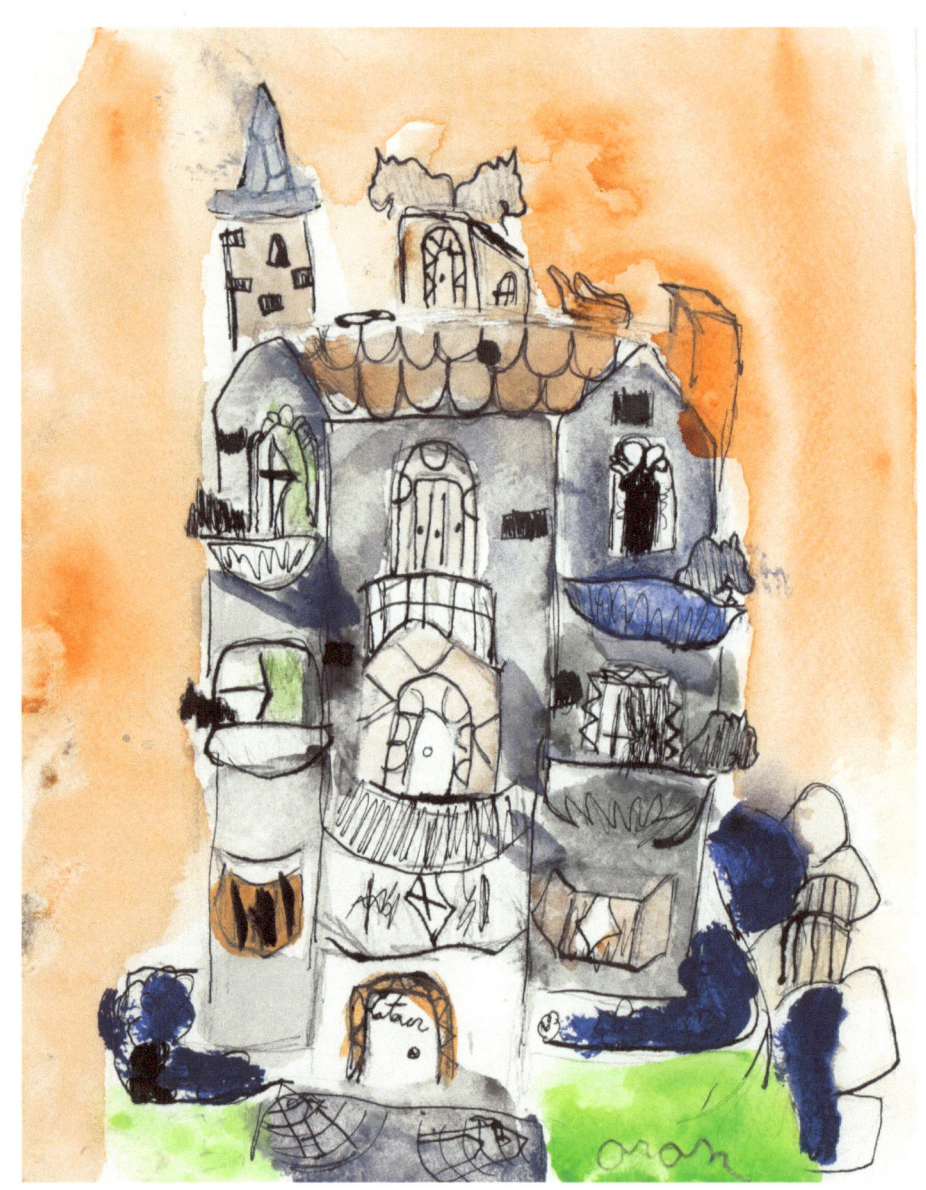

Oron Tal's Dream House
Watercolor and ink on paper, 12 x 9 inches
2011
Courtesy of Carly Weinberg

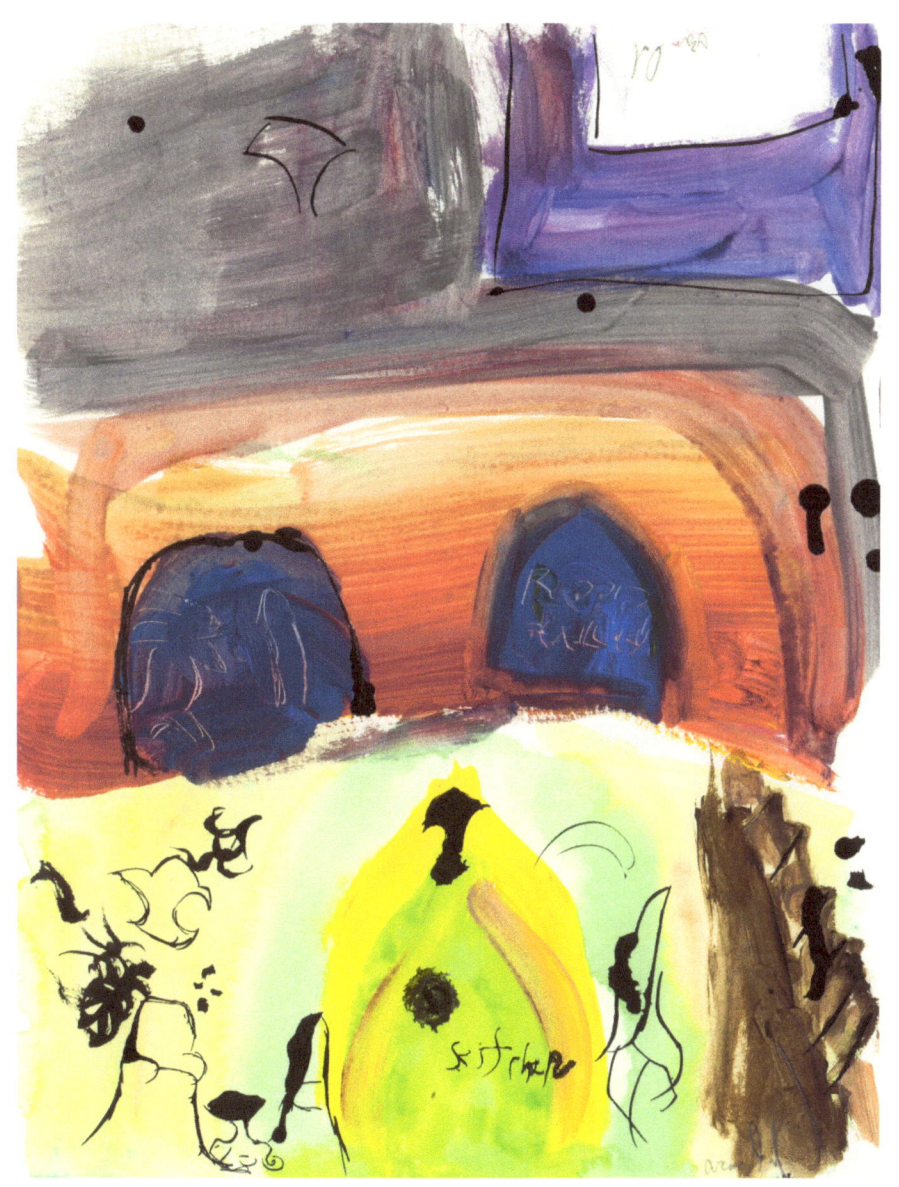

Imaginary House
Watercolor and ink on paper, 11.5 x 9 inches
2010
Courtesy of Esther Davidson

Purple Giraffe (detail)

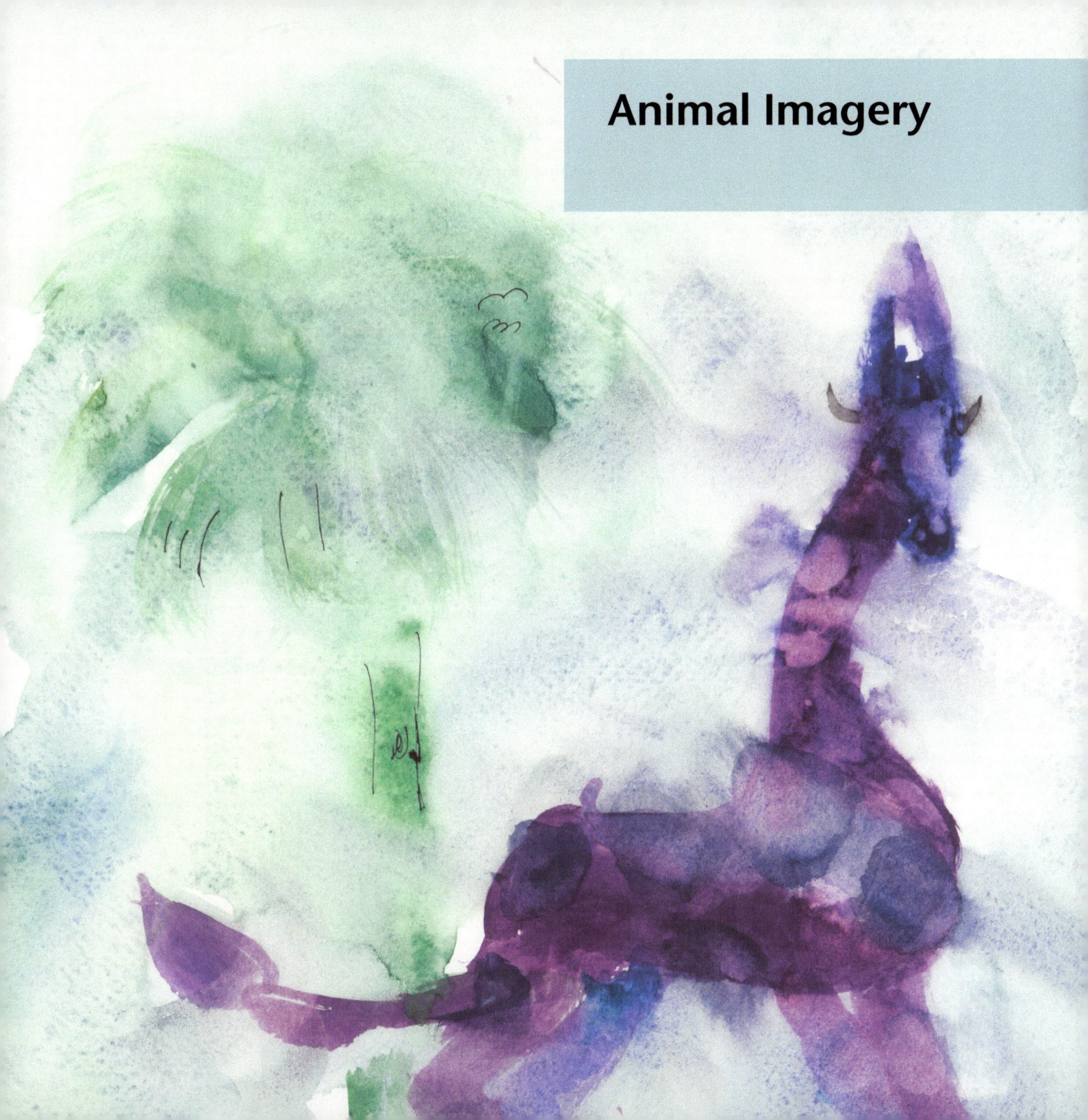

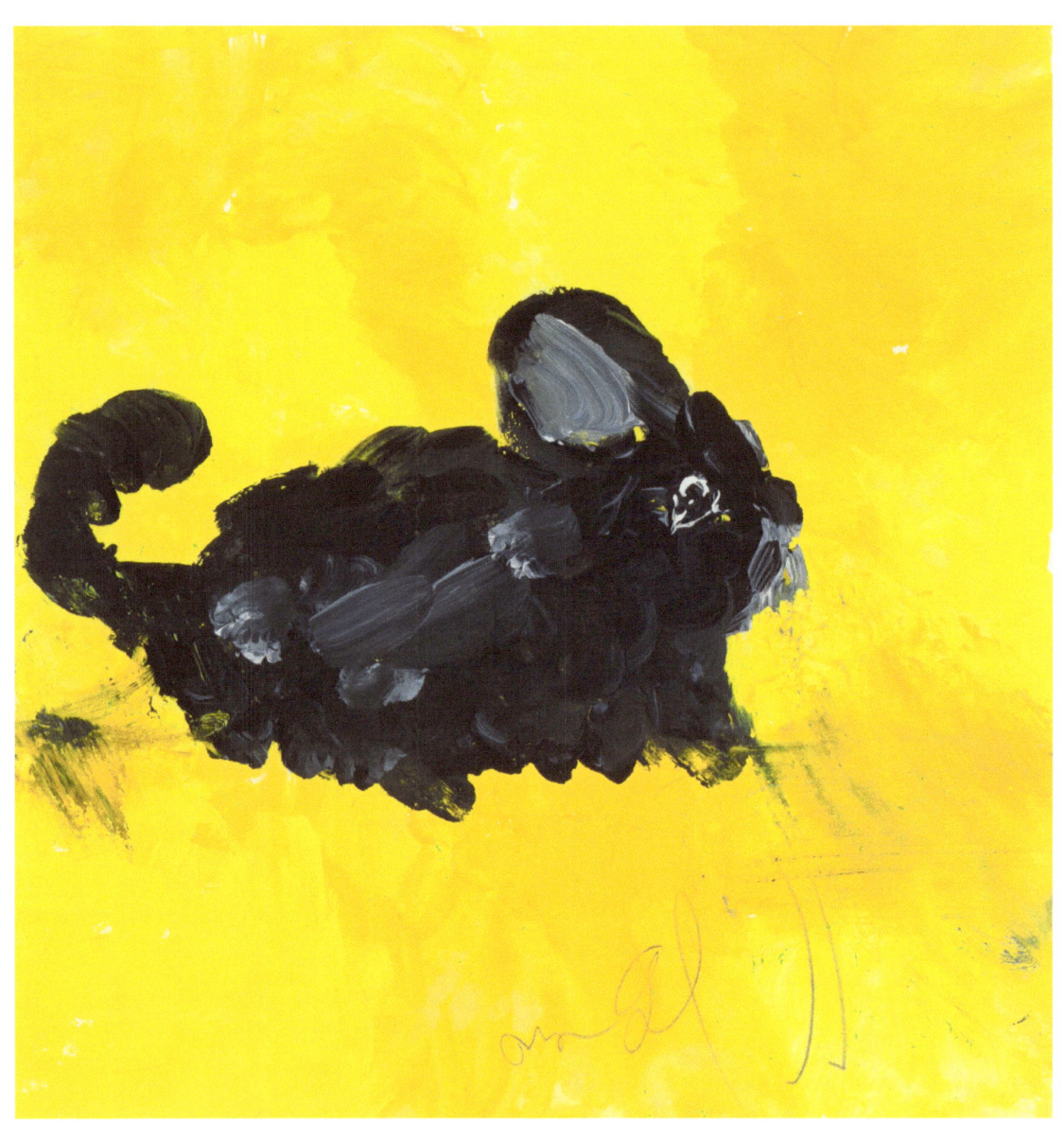

Babka
Acrylic on paper, 7 x 6.5 inches
2011
Courtesy of Gail Bach

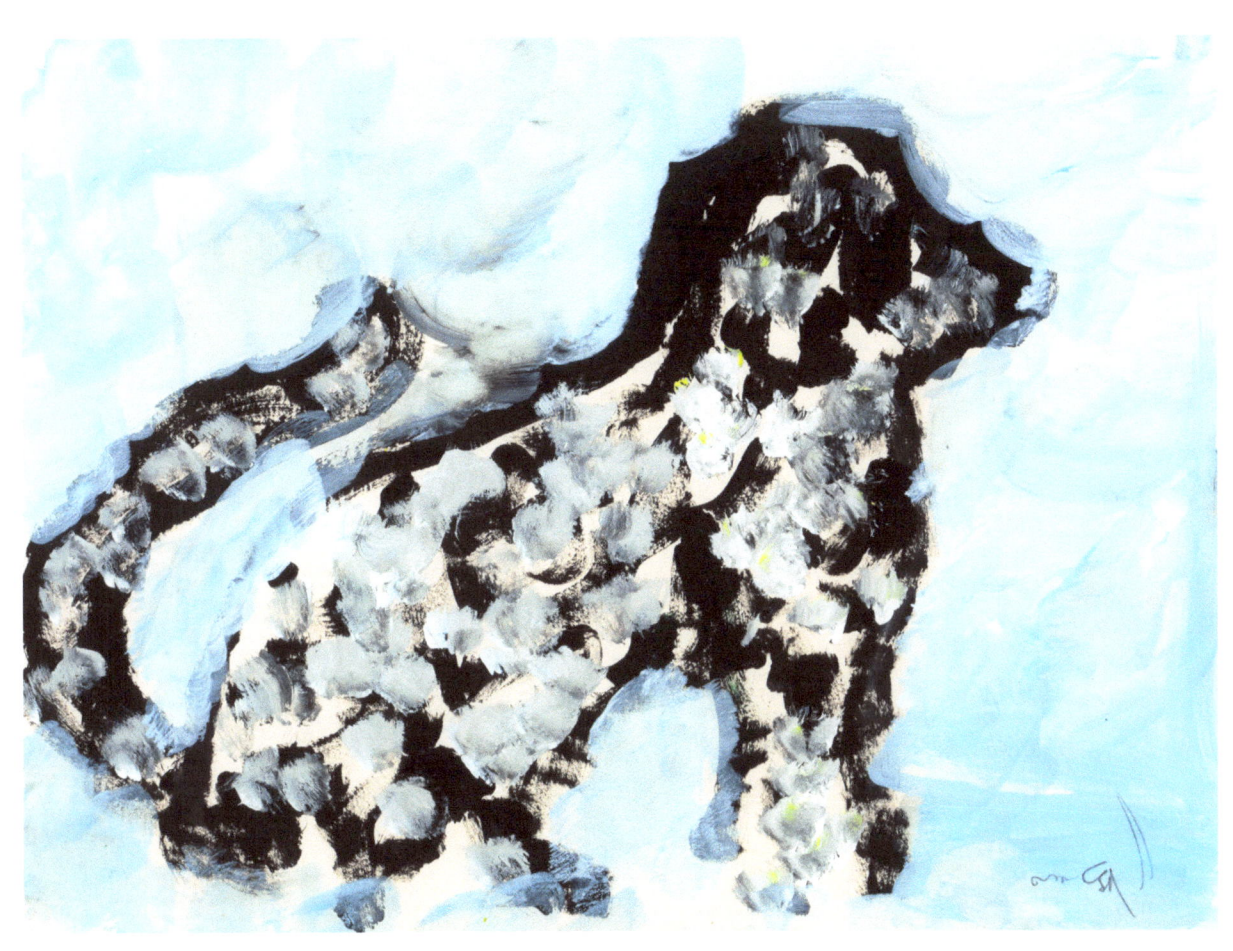

Tiger
Acrylic on paper, 9 x 12 inches
2011
Courtesy of Tyler Winter

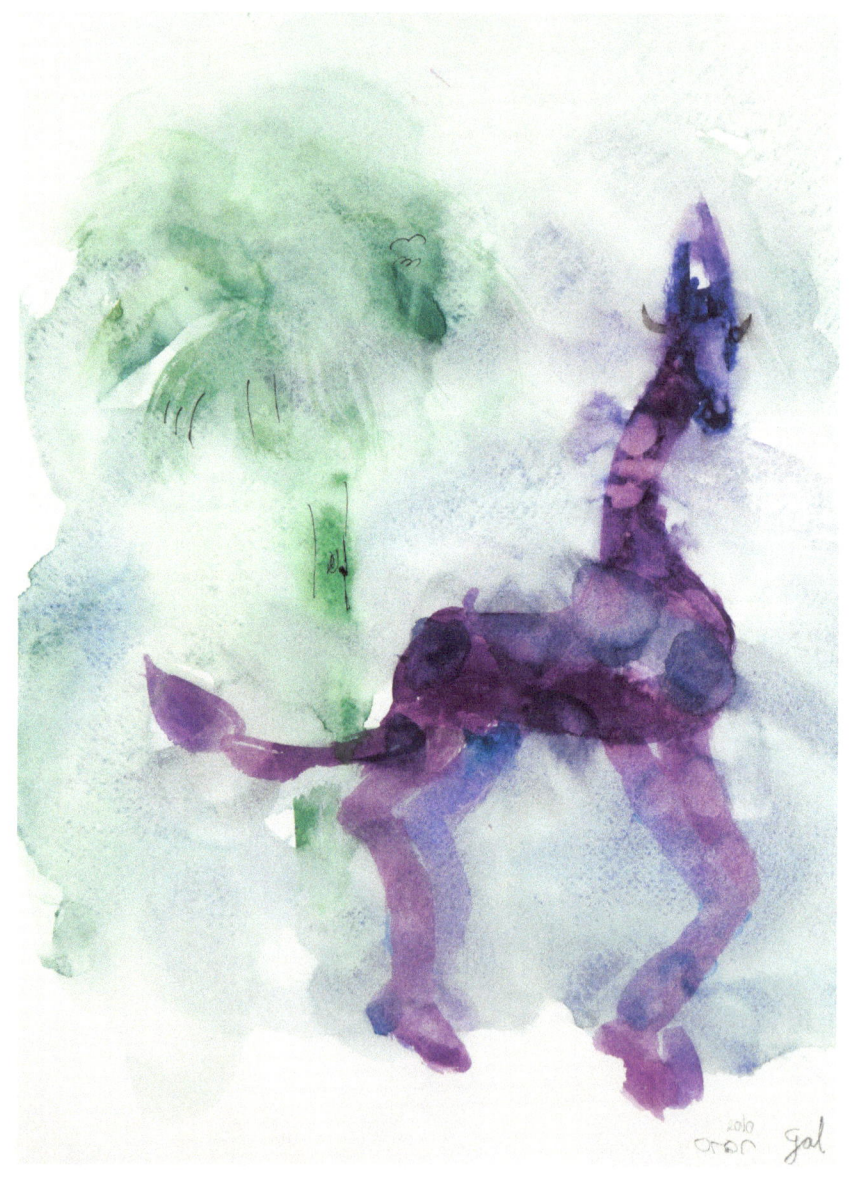

Purple Giraffe
Watercolor and ink on paper, 14 x 10.5 inches
2010
Courtesy of Oron Tal

Misty Ocean (detail)

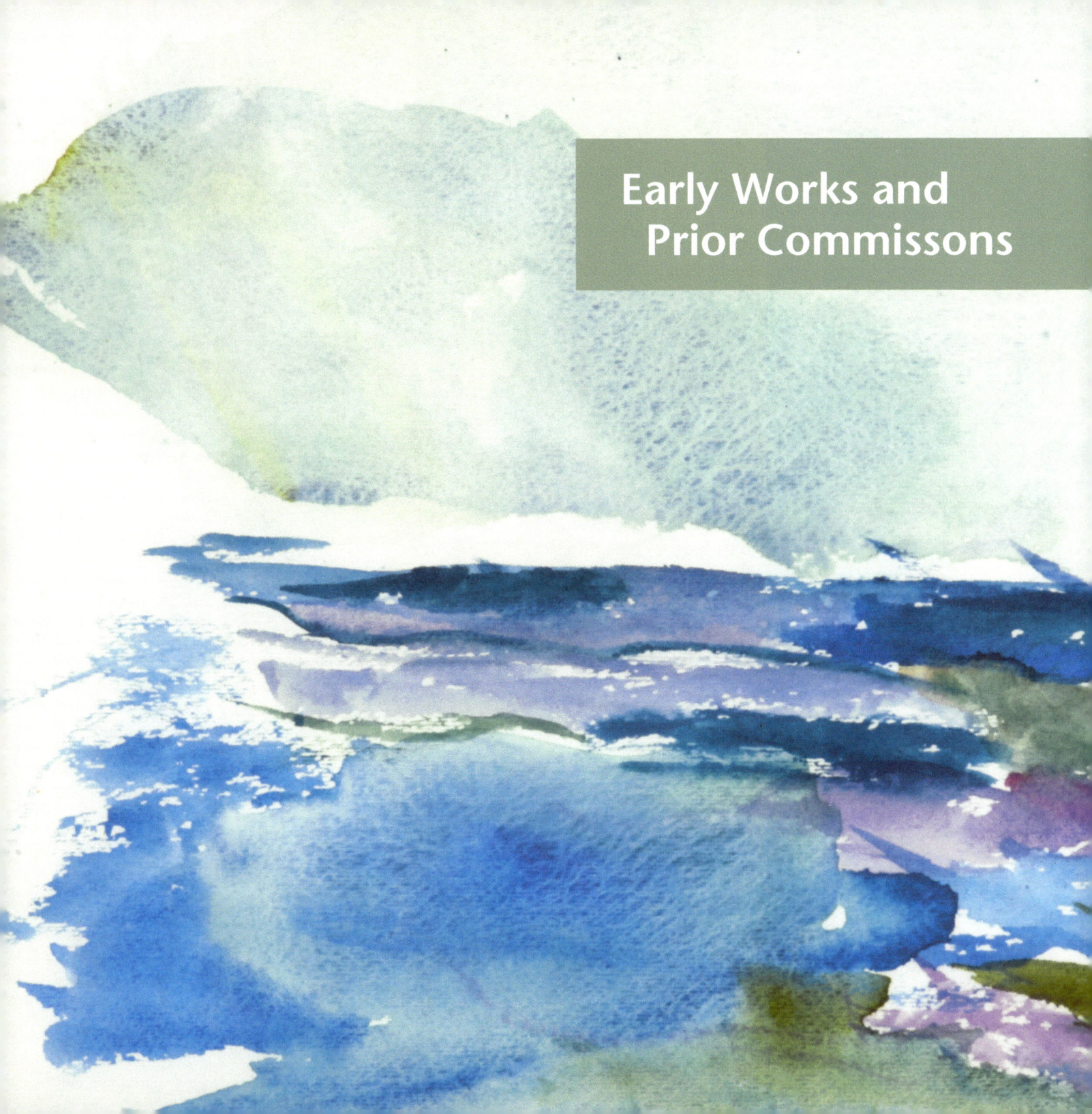

Early Works and
Prior Commissons

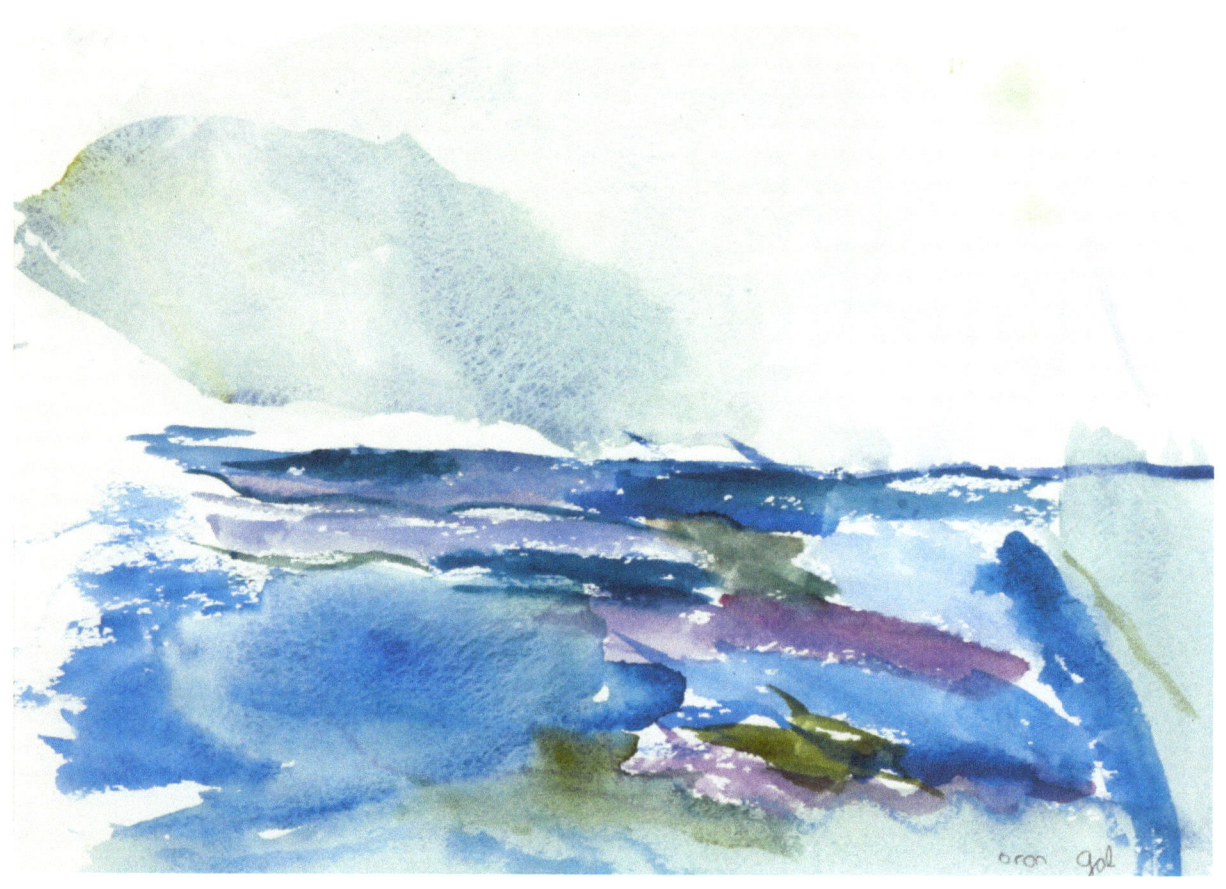

Misty Ocean
Watercolor on paper, 10.25 x 14.5 inches
2010
Courtesy of Oron Tal

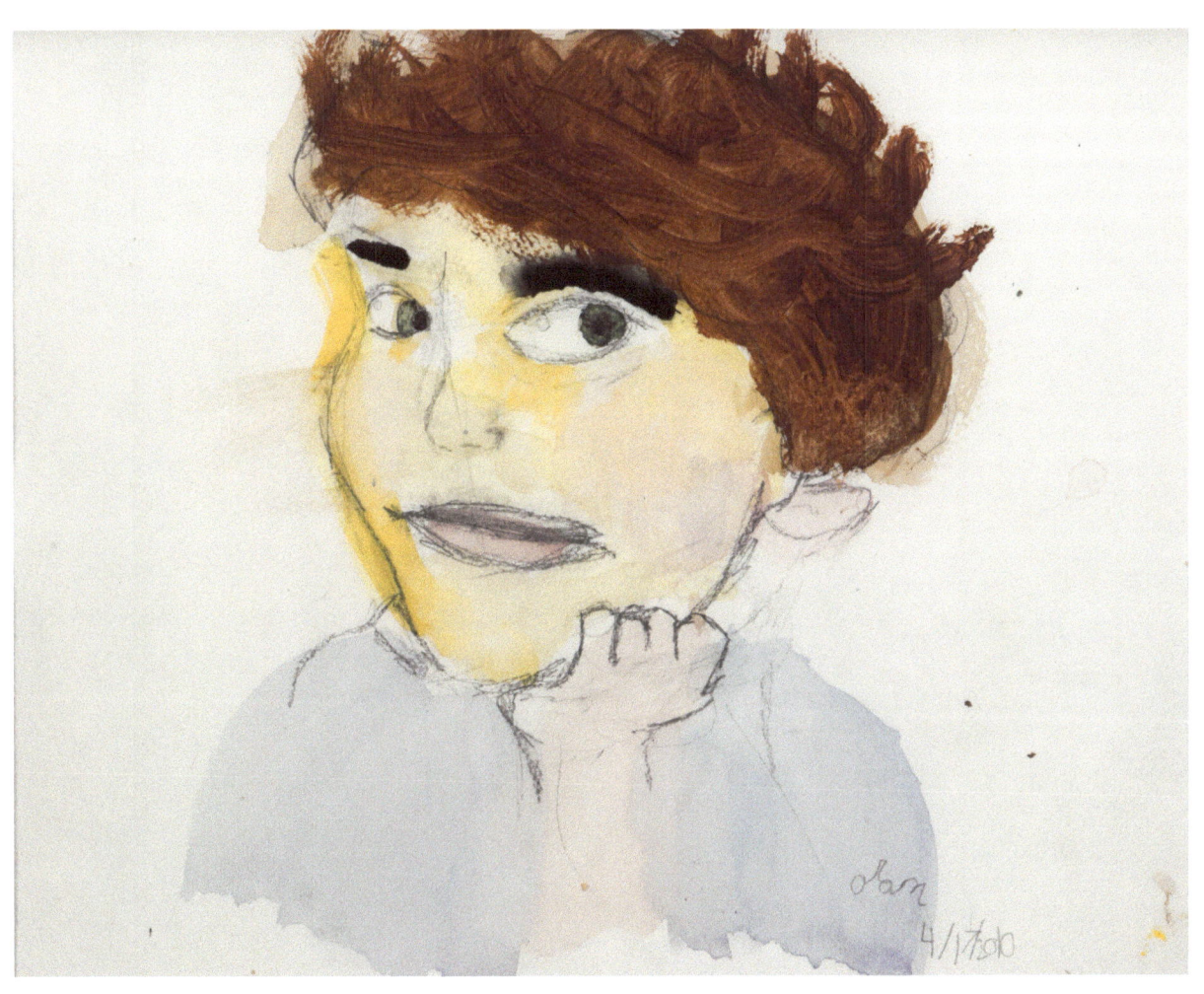

Untitled (self portrait)
Watercolor on paper, 10.5 x 13.5 inches
2010
Courtesy of Oron Tal

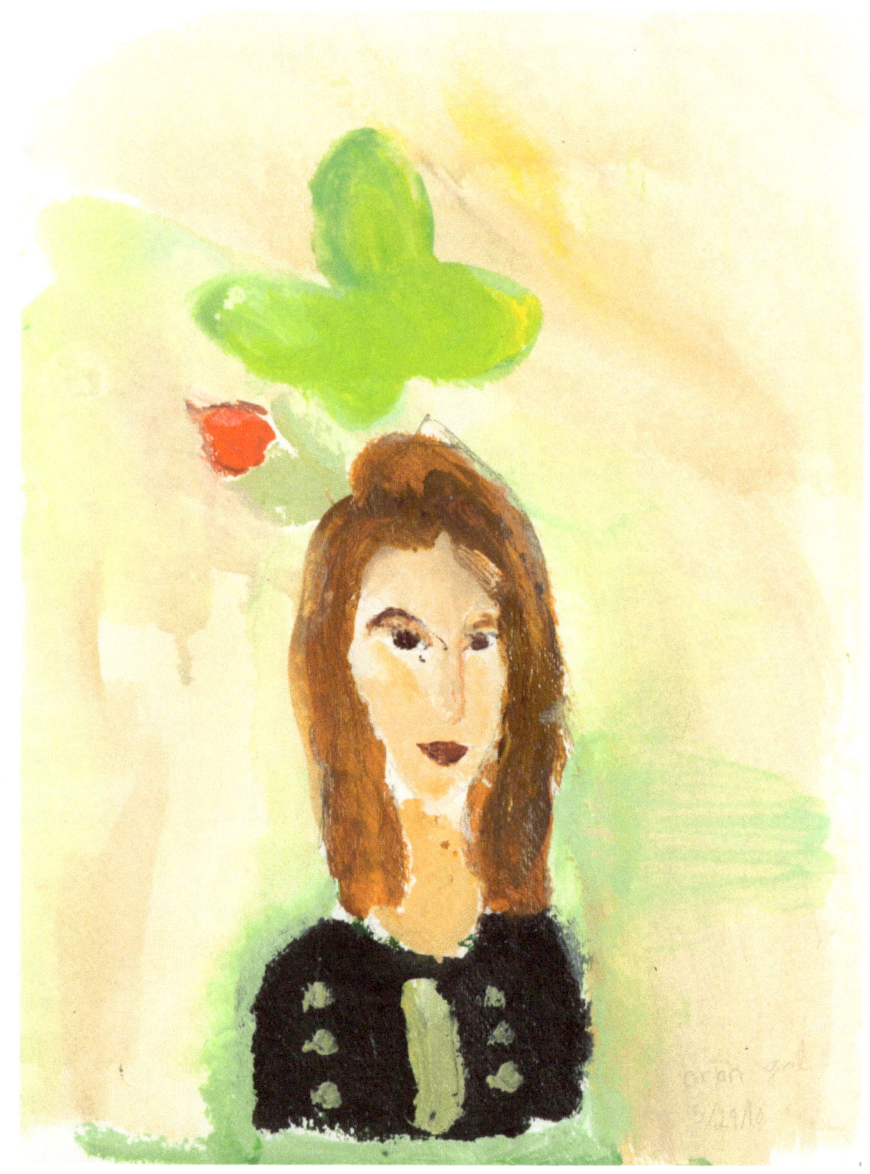

Irish Lady (after Amedeo Modigliani)
Acrylic on paper, 15 x 11 inches
2010
Courtesy of Oron Tal

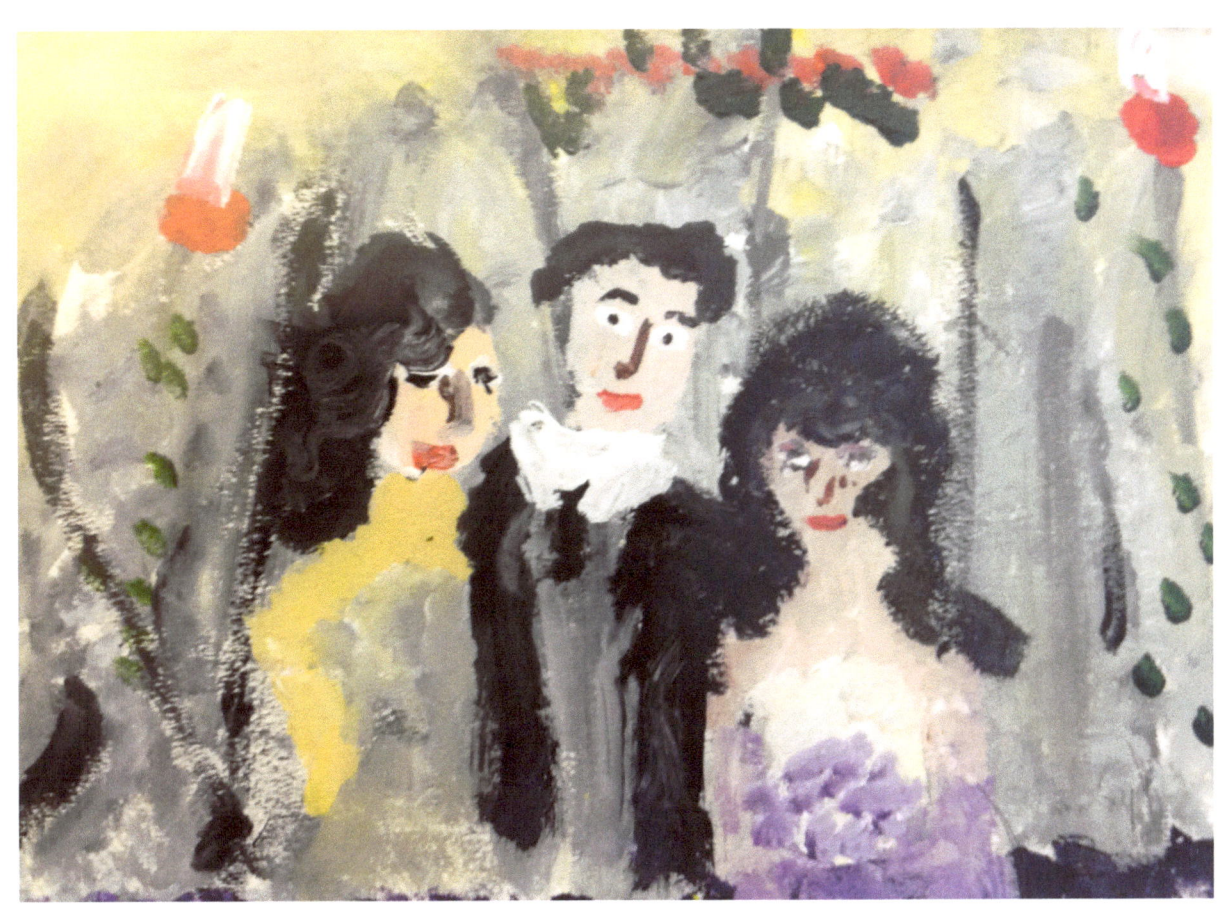

Wedding
Acrylic on paper, 10.25 x 14 inches
2011
Courtesy of Sherry and Barry Simon

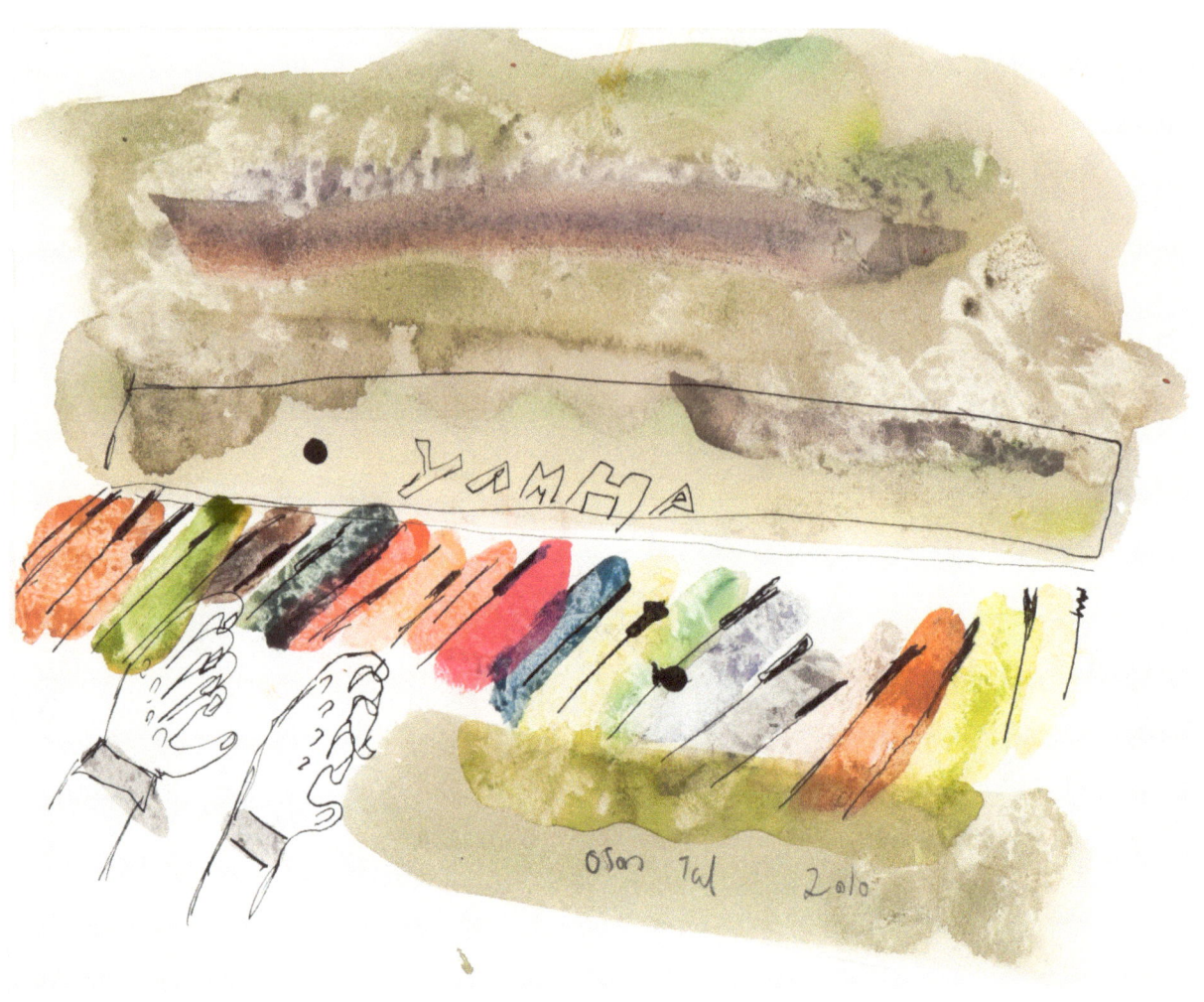

Untitled
Watercolor and ink on paper, 6.5 x 8 inches
2011
Courtesy of Yaari Nadav Tal

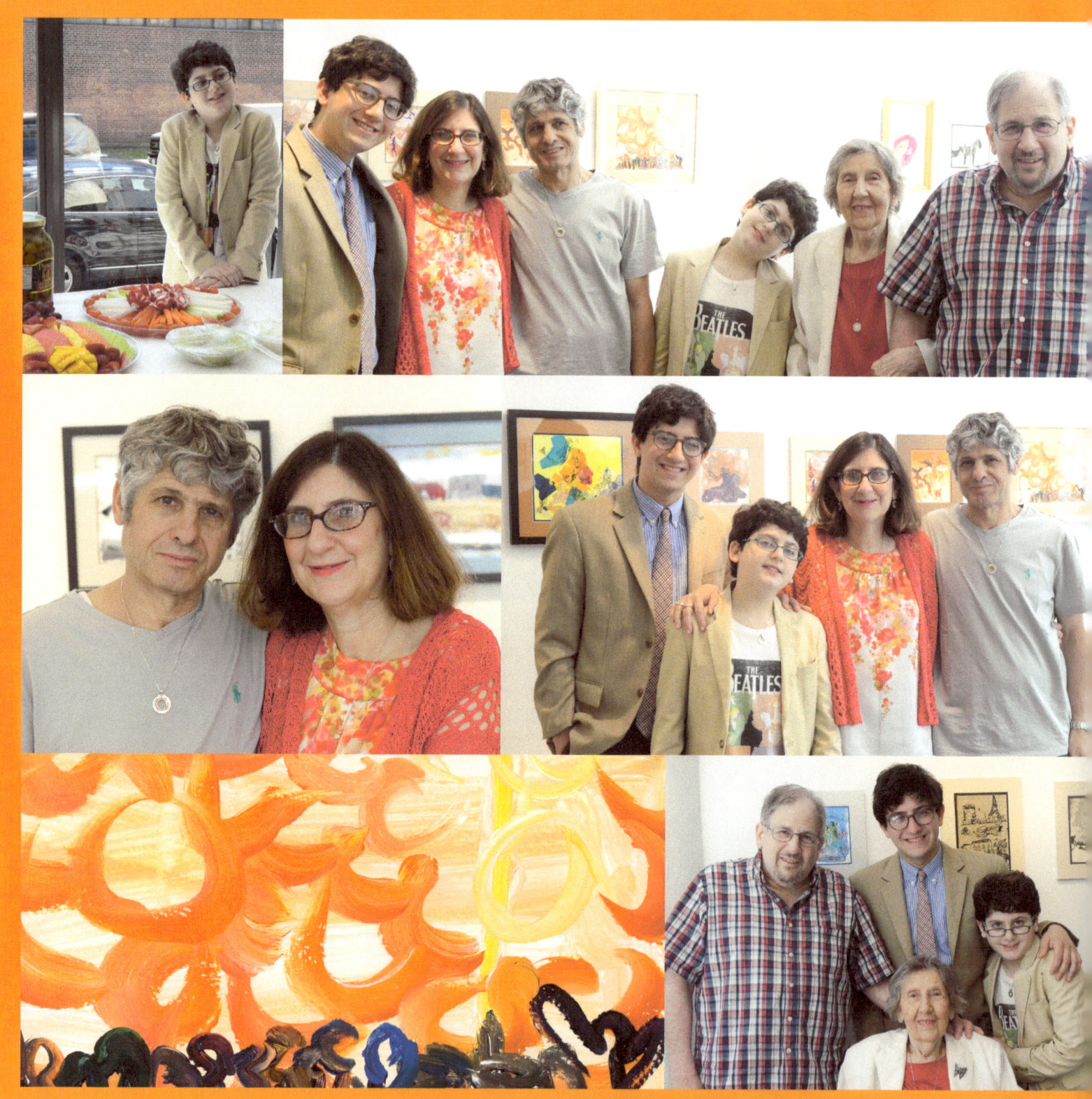

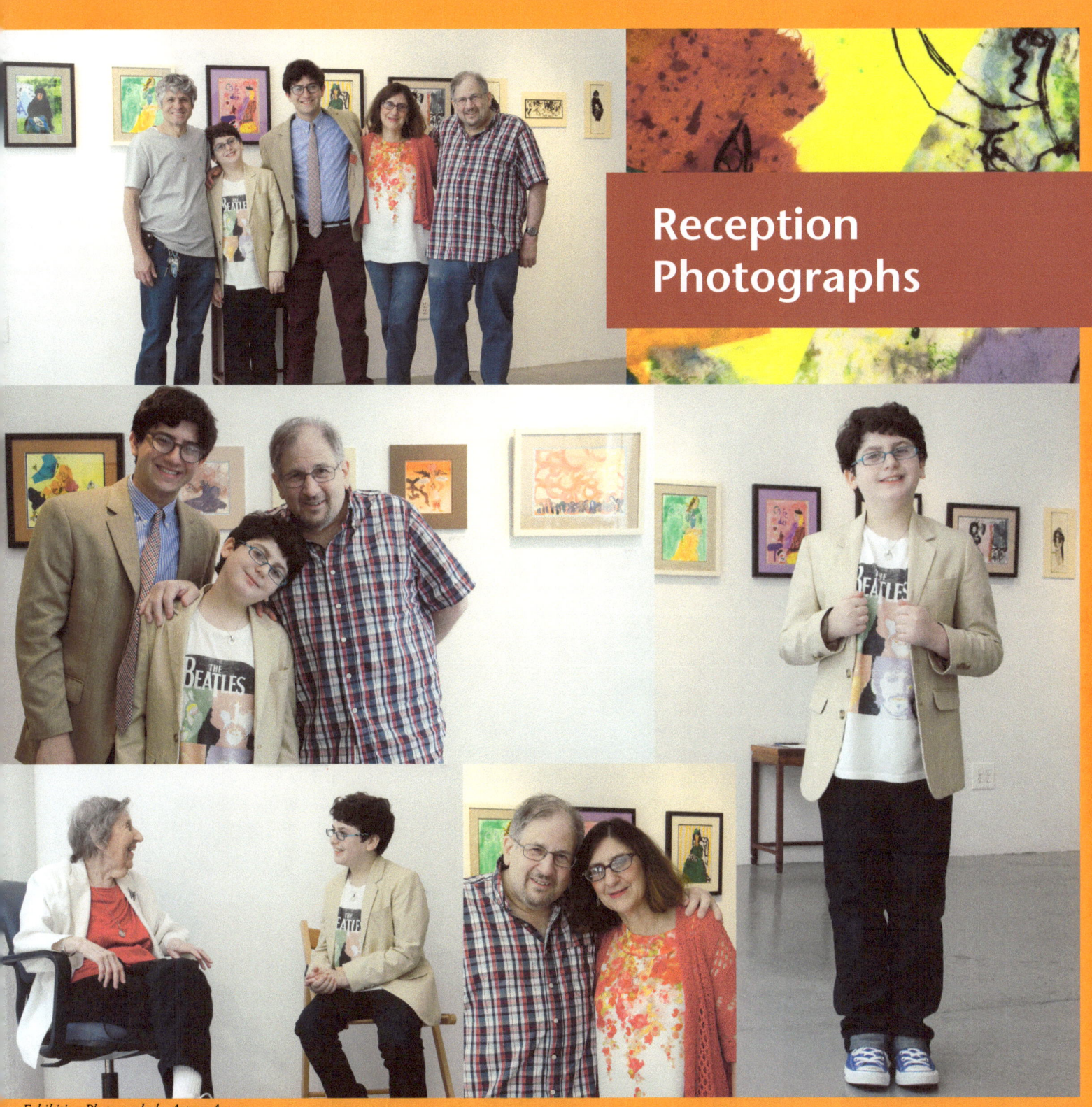

Reception Photographs

Exhibition Photographs by Arturo Amaya

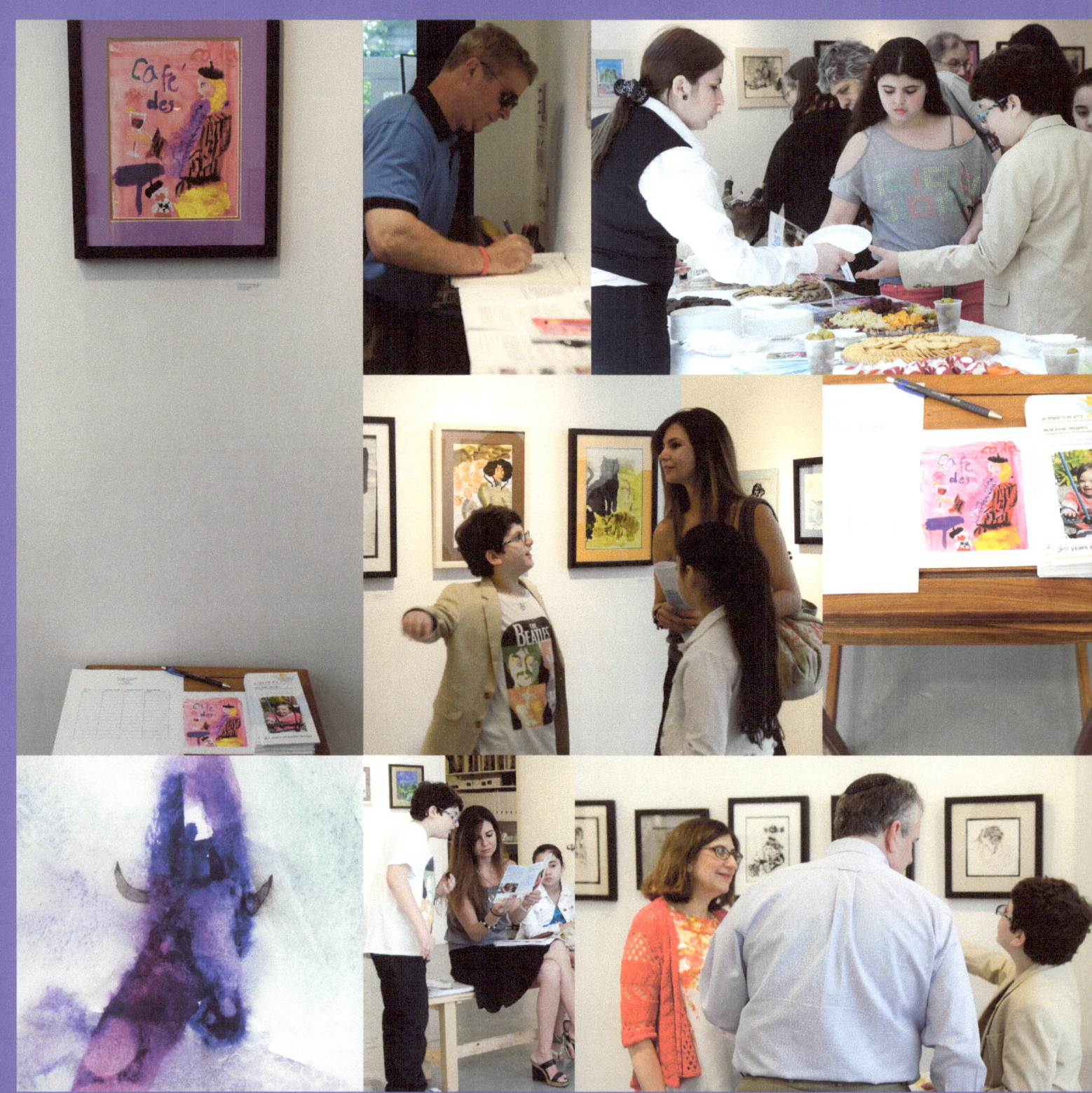

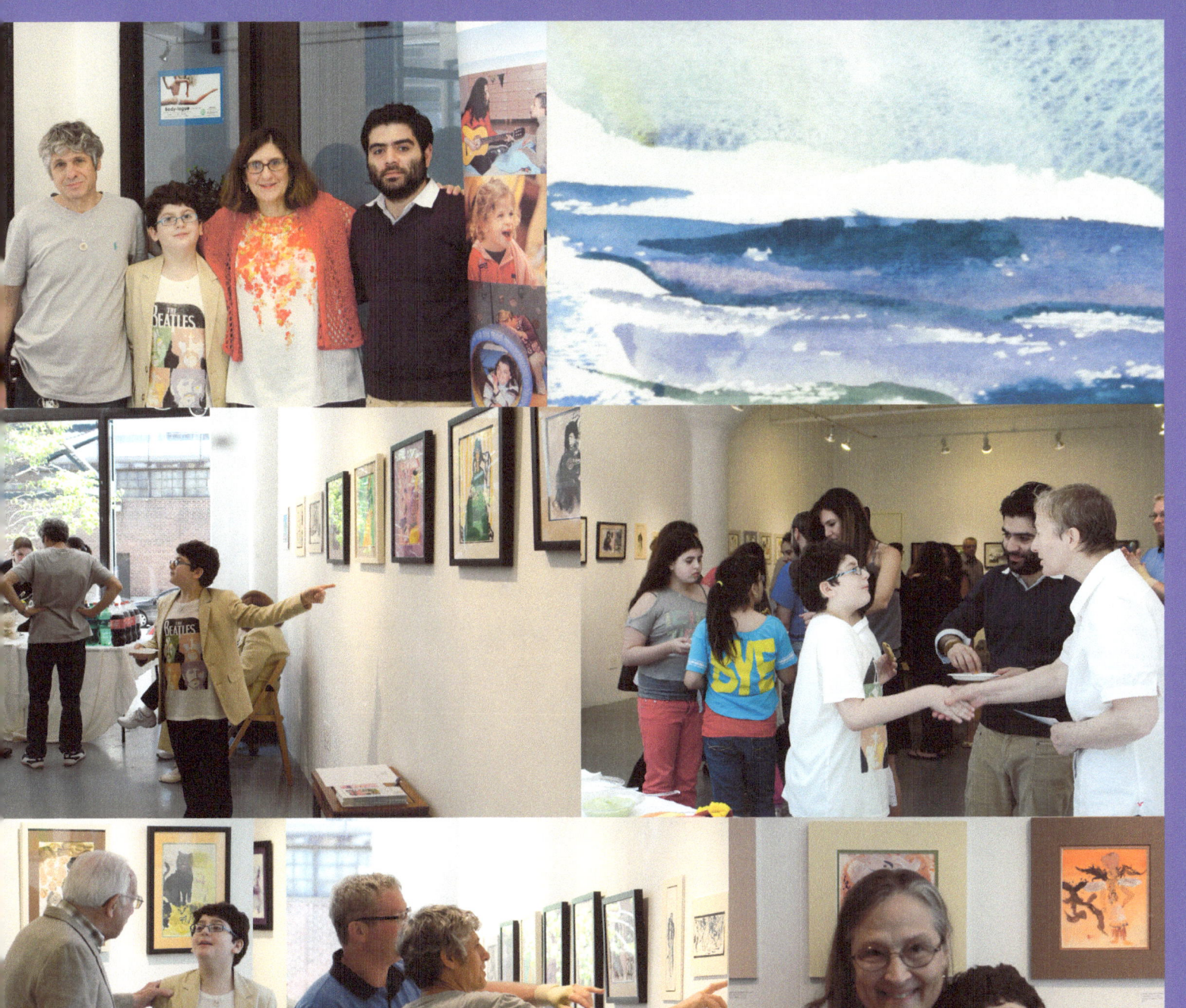

Exhibition Photographs by Arturo Amaya

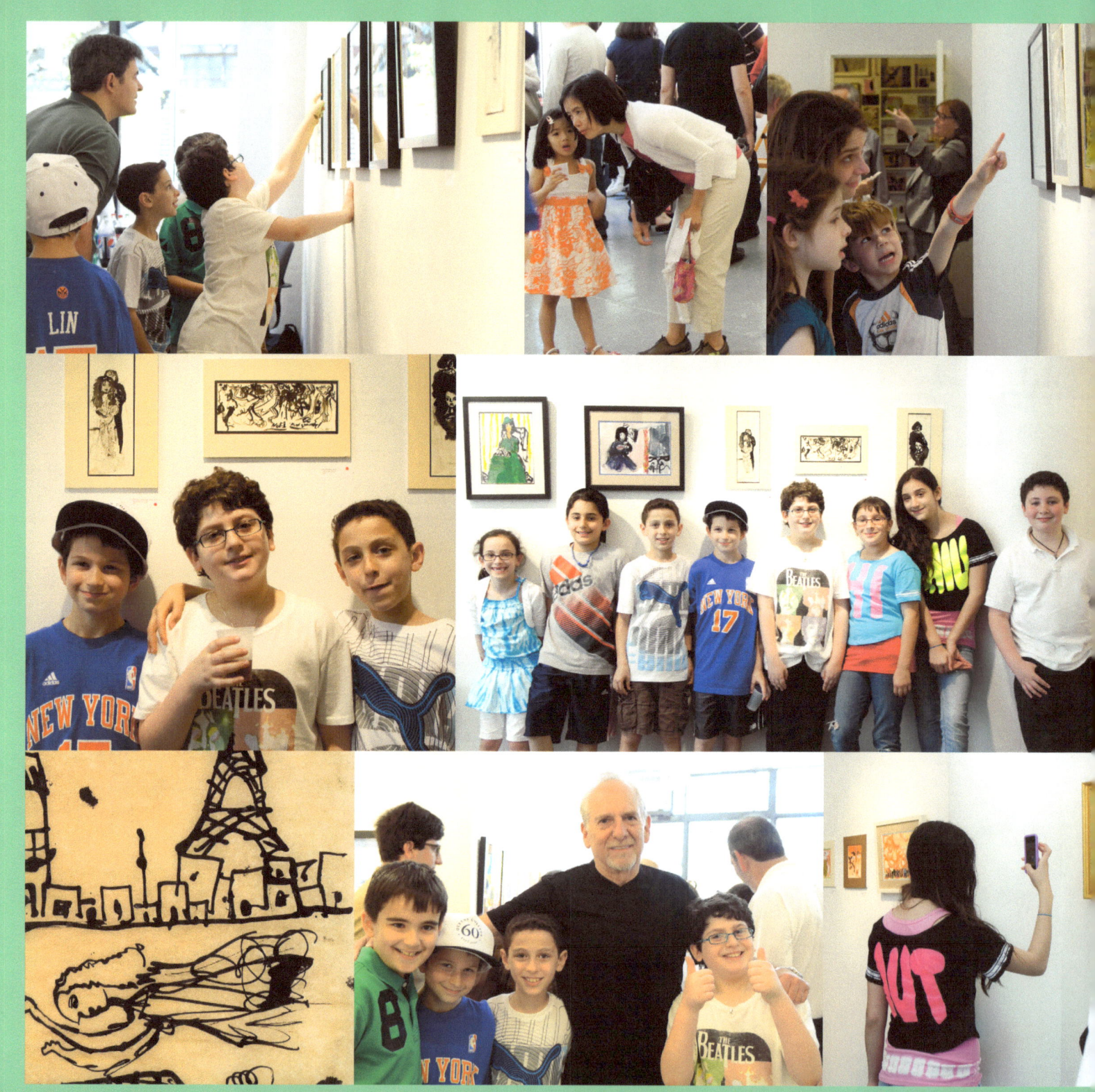

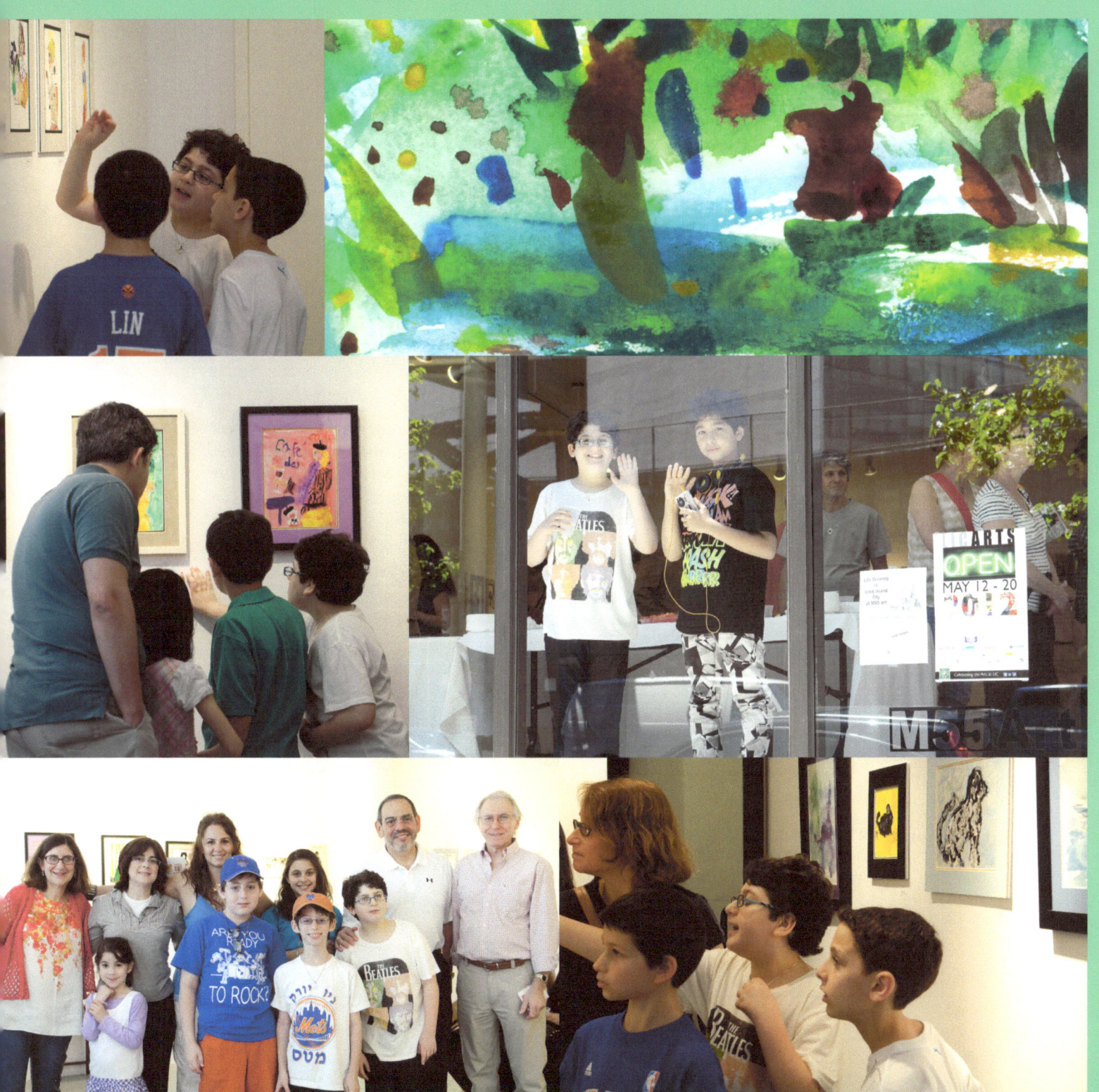

Exhibition Photographs by Arturo Amaya

Queens Chronicle

Thursday, May 17, 2012

Preteen Artist Sells Art for Good Cause

by Josey Bartlett, qboro Editor

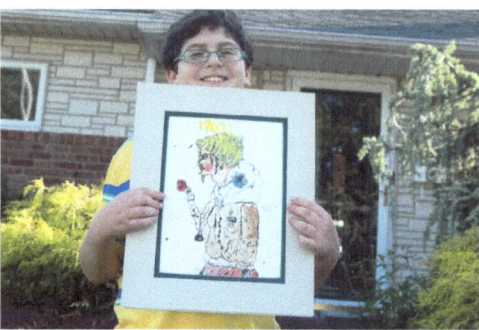

Oron Tal, 11, shows off one of the many paintings featured in Saturday's show.

Budding artist Oron Tal, 11, will exhibit his first solo show during the LIC Arts Open. Tal, a fifth grader at the Solomon Schechter School of Queens, is bubbly, talkative, sure headed — he knows what he wants and can create a painting in about 20 minutes to an hour — and a bit fidgety.

He comes from an artistic family; his father creates carved wooden sculptures and his sister works as a fashion designer.

The exhibition titled "11" Paintings and Drawings, 2010-2012, will be held in the M55 Gallery on Sunday from noon to 6 p.m.

Tal will donate proceeds from the sale of his framed artwork, priced from $100 to $200, to Beit Issie Shapiro, a nonprofit organization in Israel focusing on new therapies for children and adults with disabilities. The Tals, who live in Hollis Hills, visited the nonprofit last summer.

"I like to help out," Tal said.

"Oron's act of tzedakah [charity] is not only very meaningful in the Jewish tradition, but also illustrates the growing awareness and increase in youth philanthropy," executive director of The American Friends of Beit Issie Shapiro, Irma Friedman said.

The fifth grader started working with artist Valentina DuBasky in 2010 when he was 8. DuBasky has shown her art in 150 exhibitions nationally and internationally. She is also the founder and executive director of Art-in-a-Box, an international nonprofit.

Tal works with paint, clay and pencil — though his work on Saturday will showcase his paintings and ink pieces called nib work. His artwork is cute, playful and brightly colored. The young artist draws from his experiences, said his mother, Marcia Tal. Last year the family took a trip to Paris, where Tal gleaned inspiration for a few paintings of cafes and Parisians. One of his paintings depicts a fashionable talk show host with a crying guest.

"People in talk shows are always crying," Tal said.

He paints the things he likes such as his brother's friend's chinchilla, Babka; his dog, Tiger; and colorful people, outrageous fashion and the pop star who embodies both those things, Lady Gaga. Additionally he often likes to imagine his subject matter.

"I make people up," Tal said. "You can do whatever you want with their faces."

He's learning how to deal with little mistakes. The painting shown here was destined for the trash, said his mother, but with a little prodding from DuBasky, Tal turned an ink blot gone awry into a lock of hair on the far side of the subject's face.

"Mistakes can turn into masterpieces," Tal said.

11: Paintings and Drawings
When: May 20, noon to 6 p.m.
Where: M55 Gallery, 44-02 23 St., LIC
Tickets: Free; paintings are for sale
M55art.org, (718) 729-2988

Oron Tal "11" Exhibition

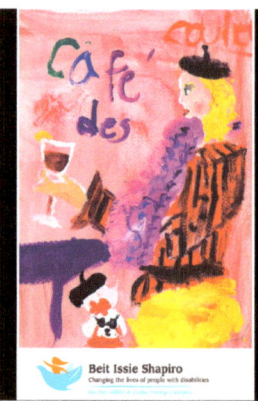 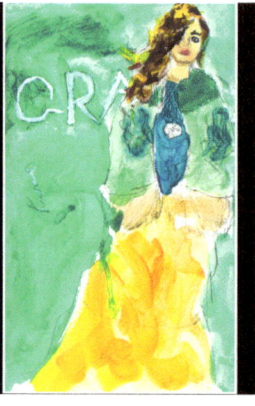

Artist Valentina DuBasky presents her student, Oron Tal, age 11, in his first solo exhibition. In 2010, Valentina accepted Oron, then an eight year old student, after recognizing his passion for art. For two years, he has been coming to Valentina's painting studio in the West Village in New York City for weekly art lessons. This exhibition marks Oron's first two years of art study with a selection of paintings and drawings in a variety of media on the themes of travel, reading, media, fashion and family.

Valentina is an exhibiting artist whose work has been included in more than 150 exhibitions nationally and internationally. She is also the founder and Executive Director of Art-in-a-Box, an international nonprofit organization. Oron's artwork has been influenced through a combination of Valentina's unique expertise, Oron's diverse experiences, his rich imagination and love of learning. Oron writes of his relationship to art:

"Art of any kind makes me feel happy and excited. In fact every day I make sketches of nature, places and people I imagine. I get pleasure in designing the facial expressions, hair and clothing of these people. Occasionally, these sketches are developed into paintings, drawings, and nib work. Many of my own experiences become part of my work."

Oron Tal is a student at Solomon Schechter School of Queens. Oron's academic environment is a place where curiosity rules and where children learn to honor timeless traditions and think for themselves. The students are encouraged to become global citizens – the classroom is a launching pad that enables students to view the world from an extraordinary new perspective. Oron's artwork projects his global lens and the recognition that we are all part of something greater than ourselves.

Being a global citizen encompasses a commitment to social responsibility – a call-to-action as compassionate human beings. Oron will be donating proceeds from the sale of his artwork to Beit Issie Shapiro, Israel's most effective nonprofit organization in 2012. Beit Issie Shapiro is a leading innovator of new therapies for children and adults with disabilities, sharing best practices internationally. Beit Issie plays a leading role in promoting the inclusion of people with disabilities in society. Oron is happy that his art can help people in need and invites all to join him in supporting Beit Issie Shapiro.

Oron's show, "11" Paintings and Drawings, 2010-2012, presents 50 original works of art that demonstrate the breadth and depth of Oron's creativity, intellect and skill in expressing his ideas and interpreting the world around him. Please join us to celebrate the beginning of a unique creative journey of a young artist.

The Queens Courier

May, 2012

Oron Tal "11" – Paintings and Drawings

11 year old Oron Tal visited a center treating children and adults with cognitive and development disabilities in Israel. He was so moved by the program and what he saw, he decided to raise as much money as possible by selling his paintings to support the charity. Oron said, "I am so happy that my artwork can help such a great place!!"

Oron will be showing his art work at M55ART – 44-02 23rd Street, Long Island City, New York during the "LI Arts Open" on Sunday May 20, 2012 from 12:00pm – 6:00pm

Oron, who lives in Hollis Hills, Queens with his parents, is in the fifth grade at the Solomon Schechter School in Queens. He started painting as a young child and began lessons at 8 years old. He has four older siblings of which two live in Israel, one is studying in Israel at the Sackler School of Medicine and one is studying at George Washington University

A portion of the proceeds from the sale of the artwork will go to Beit Issie Shapiro, a non-profit organization that is a leader and innovator of new therapies for children and adults with disabilities in Israel.

Beit Issie Shapiro was named Israel's most effective nonprofit organization in 2011-2012. A leading innovator of new therapies for children and adults with disabilities, over the past 30 years the organization has grown from serving 16 children with developmental disabilities to impacting on some 30,000 people every year. Beit Issie Shapiro helps train thousands of therapists in Israel in its new therapies, conducts research and shares best practice internationally. Beit Issie Shapiro plays a leading role in promoting the inclusion of people with disabilities in society and advocating for better legal provisions for people with disabilities.

Date: Sunday, May 20th
Time: 12:00PM - 6:00PM
Location: M55ART – 44-02 23rd Street, Long Island City, New York
Oron Tal is available for interviews prior to the exhibit.

FIOS 1 Long Island

May, 2012

Art Exhibit To Benefit Special Needs Children's Charity In Israel

11 year old Oron Tal visited a center treating children and adults with cognitive and development disabilities in Israel. He was so moved by the program and what he saw, he decided to raise as much money as possible by selling his paintings to support the charity. Oron said, "I am so happy that my artwork can help such a great place!"

Oron will be showing his art work at M55ART – 44-02 23rd Street, Long Island City, New York during the "LI Arts Open" on Sunday May 20, 2012 from 12:00pm – 6:00pm.

Oron, who lives in Hollis Hills, Queens with his parents, is in the fifth grade at the Solomon Schechter School in Queens. He started painting as a young child and began lessons at 8 years old. He has four older siblings of which two live in Israel, one is studying in Israel at the Sackler School of Medicine and one is studying at George Washington University.

A portion of the proceeds from the sale of the artwork will go to Beit Issie Shapiro, a non-profit organization that is a leader and innovator of new therapies for children and adults with disabilities in Israel.

Beit Issie Shapiro was named Israel's most effective nonprofit organization in 2011-2012. A leading innovator of new therapies for children and adults with disabilities, over the past 30 years the organization has grown from serving 16 children with developmental disabilities to impacting on some 30,000 people every year. Beit Issie Shapiro helps train thousands of therapists in Israel in its new therapies, conducts research and shares best practice internationally. Beit Issie Shapiro plays a leading role in promoting the inclusion of people with disabilities in society and advocating for better legal provisions for people with disabilities.

INDEX OF COLOR PLATES

www.ingramcontent.com/pod-product-compliance
Lightning Source LLC
Chambersburg PA
CBHW050723180526
45159CB00003B/1112